Praise for

KAREN ELIZABETH GORDON

"Eerily sensitive to the creative potential of language, Karen Elizabeth Gordon has birthed a genre and renewed the language." —Robert Grudin

"Karen Elizabeth Gordon does in words what Edward Gorey does in drawings: she presents a neat, mandarin order that can't keep out—indeed, almost invites—intrusions of the bizarre." —*Newsweek*

"I can think of no one whose life and language would not be brightened by any and all of Gordon's work." —*Baltimore Sun*

"Gordon's books are compassion-filled little lighthouses among language's treacherous shoals." —*Sacramento Bee*

"The chief delight in Gordon's work is not so much the information she imparts . . . Rather it is in watching as she rubs words together to conjure wildly imaginative and cleverly suggestive sentences." —*Los Angeles Times Book Review*

"How rare it is to laugh as one studies a grammar text." —Doris Grumbach, National Public Radio

"Let Ms. Gordon rewrite all the school textbooks and we'll have the most literate population in the world." —Charles Simic

"Miss Gordon manages to make the period, question mark, exclamation point, comma, and semicolon sound friendly instead of forbidding . . . Such sentences might make the Edwardian Brothers Fowler blush and, perhaps, Professor Strunk and Mr. White wince." —*New York Times*

"Gordon's saucy crash courses are short on pedantry and long on wit." —*Virginian-Pilot*

Other books by Karen Elizabeth Gordon

The Disheveled Dictionary

A Curious Caper
Through Our Sumptuous Lexicon

Karen Elizabeth Gordon

A MARINER BOOK
Houghton Mifflin Company
Boston   New York

For Steven Moore

First Mariner Books edition 2003

Copyright © 1997 by Karen Elizabeth Gordon

For information about permission to reproduce selections from this book, write to Permissions, Houghton Mifflin Company, 215 Park Avenue South, New York, New York 10003.

Visit our Web site: www.houghtonmifflinbooks.com.

Library of Congress Cataloging-in-Publication Data .

Gordon, Karen Elizabeth.
   The disheveled dictionary : a curious caper through our sumptuous lexicon / Karen Elizabeth Gordon.
      p. cm.
   ISBN 0-395-68990-2
   ISBN 0-618-38196-1 (pbk.)
   1. English language—Glossaries, vocabularies, etc.
2. Vocabulary.   I. Title.
PE1583.G67   1997
423—dc21   97-2985   CIP

Book design by Anne Chalmers

Printed in the United States of America

QUM 10 9 8 7 6 5 4 3 2 1

Acknowledgments and credit lines begin on page 159.

A Preface from Yolanta

Just returned from the American Wild West, I was washing the dust and vermin from my hair in one of Amplochacha's public fountains when another pair of hands crept over my skull and tugged my torso upright (surely some half-drowned vermin disappearing down the stranger's sleeves). Facing my assailant, I recognized The Author, surrounded by exploding luggage and with a ticket clenched in her teeth. "I'm off to France," she said, thrusting the ticket between *my* teeth so she could talk and I couldn't, the strangest kiss I've ever received, "and you have to write the preface." Snatching the ticket back, thumping me on the head with her passport, and yanking my frothy ringlets in farewell (see *gossamer*), she abandoned me and the manuscript to the silence of that city square. Her notes for the introduction, what's more, I later found in my hip pocket—seventy pages, no less, which I have put out of their misery with a match. I should say that I am used to such treatment and am addicted to its rewards; I comply after my own fashion and in my own sweet time.

Yes, it *is* sweet, just like frangipane the pastry and frangipani the scent. Did you know that frangipani takes its name from an Italian count who distilled the flower of the red jasmine to perfume his gloves?

The name was only later applied to *crème à la frangipane*, an almond-infused *délice* that gives its name to Café Frangipane, which you shall visit soon. But Frangipani is also the name of the dummy from whose muslin body some of this book's sentences were plundered: the darling mute is losing weight as she surrenders fragments of *Pierrot and the Whiplash, The Abduction of the Magi, Torpor in the Swing, The Glasnost Menagerie, The Wretch of Lugubria, To Die in a Dirndl,* and *The Stupor of Flanelle Lune.* For The Author, this tailor's dummy embodies the paradox—half ardor, half torment—that haunts her waking hours: How ineffable are our feelings and experience, yet what have we but our language to make sense of our senses stirred?

Constanza, the contralto who makes such a racket here, would say, "Ah, but music is the key to it all," and I suspect that her voice is so insistent, her appearance so frequent for precisely that reason. This tremulous temptress of a dictionary is about the music of language, the sound and sensuality of words, the rhythms and cadences they embrace, affecting us on several levels at once. How *all* the words behave together in these passages is what matters, not merely the meaning of this or that vaguely apprehended word being defined in one place and used again in another context. This is truly cause for applause—words' acrobatic agility and changeability, their energetic grace. The more ample one's lexicon, the more supple one's thought, the more daring, charged, engaged. Frangipani and frangipane evoke the fragrance and taste of these potent little packages, these scripted symbols of our minds. It's a short hop from sensuality to metaphor, the figurative use of words, and a tribute to this pleasure you will find under *concatenation*.

This book is about liberating words from their literal meanings, ourselves from our circumscribed scripts. Come to these sentences and get into their drift; come to your senses and climb into this gift, aglimmer with palpable presences, animated with mischief and mirth. Couturière Flaumina Untergasser looses her Sumptuary Outlaw collection upon the runway of these pages as an allusion to how language can enrich our experiences and perceptions. English vaunts an especially sumptuous array of sounds and shades of meaning, having drawn from so many sources in fashioning its lexicon. *The Disheveled Dictionary* celebrates not only the less familiar, but also our most beloved and basic words.

Finding Your Way in This Book

BY JONQUIL MAPP

As my name implies, I am a geographer and cartographer, and it is as such you must take me in what follows, even though you may be remembering my antics at the Last Judgment Pinball Machine Motel. True, I am still serving my apprenticeship with the wisest man in all of Louvelandia, but I know enough to dulcify your itinerary and have promised not to distract you from this purpose by flashing you magical hinterlands in the whirl of my skirts. *Dulcify*, to initiate this elucidation properly, you will find under *D*, not long before the lurid account of my *effrontery*.

Need I iterate that you proceed from *A* to *Z*? It's not a tough alphabet to follow. Ah, but I know all about roving eyes, exploring hands, and far be it from me to suggest yours be otherwise. Stray, amble, alight where you please. You *will* be pleased, for wherever you land, you'll encounter fond acquaintances from *The New Well-Tempered Sentence*, where I too first appeared: Loona, Laurinda Moostracht (on her honeymoon), her Eurobanking uncle Nimbo, Gregor Schlaffenfuss and Flaumina Untergasser, Miranda and Mrs.

Gallimauf, the mastodons with their rough and polished manners, cowboys with their lingerie, Lada Larkovich, assorted royal riffraff, including the Duchess Ilona, and the tailor's dummy, who for the first time ever opens her mouth with a passionate interjection, and finds, at last, her name: Frangipani. In their company we return to the lands of Lavukistan, Louvelandia, Trajikistan, Azuriko, Blegue, and the city of Amplochacha. New venues (the Pink Antler Saloon, Café Frangipane, Blotto Junction) welcome us along with new characters who frequent them while also frequenting our minds: Fiona O'Flimsie, Alf Musket, Constanza Zermattress, Strophe Dulac; a chasmophile and a troglodyte; Fluriel, the Angel of Youthful Confusion; a famulus, a Rosicrucian piglet, a tomcat named Deux Chevaux, and some aggressive chocolate mousses.

But words are characters in this book too, and are, indeed, its stars. You'll meet *umbrage* in a personals ad, *fripperous* in a passage from *Menace in Venice*, while in that same city you will be led through the fog by a *cicerone*. The Grim Reaper calls on a reluctant baba to parlay the import of *internuncio*, and *extirpate* appears most incongruously with a pair of cowboy boots. As you encounter *abrogate*, *cachinnate*, *asseverate*, *quodlibet*, *thaumaturge*, *poltergeist*, *sotto voce*, *skirl*, and *Schadenfreude* amongst froufrou interiors and savage landscapes (taking a break for a bit of *dolce far niente*), you will kick off your boots, shrug off your hauteur to roll in a bed of camisoles, beside yourself with belief, at a loss for words!

Being particularly alive to place, not to mention genius loci, I feel impelled to point out that many of the words defined and in action here are of Latinate origin and multisyllabic structure, for these are the words we look up repeatedly for reassurance or precision (although ambiguity, too, has its charms). *Pajamas*, de rigueur at Café Frangipane, comes from Persia, as do many of our most beautiful sounds, which we shall one day journey to, sleeping over in a seraglio. A panegyric of our earliest English and what remains of it you will find under the mock academic entry of *gossamer*. What's most exciting, though, is not where a word has been but where it's going, what *you* will make of it, and you don't have to be a crossword puzzler or word buff (are word buffs people who play Strip Scrabble?) to amplify your own rich, raucous, sexy vocabulary, whether you wish to become a polysyllabic jazz conversationalist or to discover how words can take us beyond our meanings, exalting our very existence. Although Osip Mandelstam was speaking about poetry in his *Conversation about Dante*, I leave you with this splendid snatch of that monologue to illuminate your notion of the immense adventure our language holds for us:

> Any given word is a bundle, and meaning sticks out
> of it in various directions, not aspiring toward any
> single official point. In pronouncing the word "sun,"
> we are, as it were, undertaking an enormous jour-
> ney to which we are so accustomed that we travel in

XI

our sleep. What distinguishes poetry from automatic speech is that it rouses and shakes us into wakefulness in the middle of a word. Then it turns out that the word is much longer than we thought, and we remember that to speak means to be forever on the road.

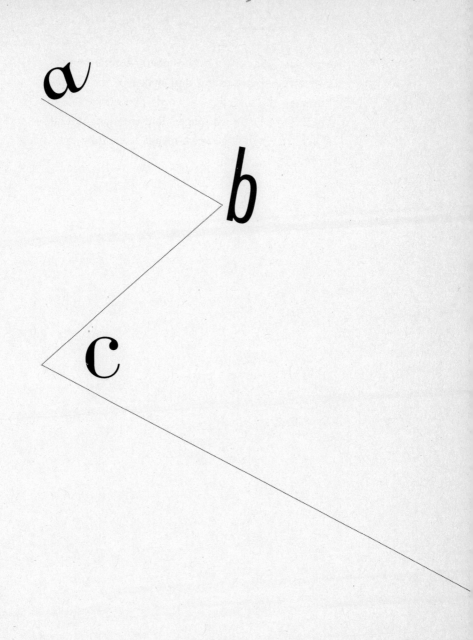

abrogate

to abolish, do away with, or annul, especially by authority

Even as a child, the prince showed a tendency to gentle derangements: at the age of four he persuaded the queen mother to abrogate Azuriko's sumptuary laws so that his imaginary playmates could wear ermine earmuffs, aureate collars of preposterous height, bejeweled knickers, dentellated tights, and musk-ox muffs and mittens.

accolade

an expression of approval, praise; special acknowledgment or award; ceremonial embrace; also, as a transitive verb, *accolade* means to praise or honor

"One week he'd invite me for drinks and humiliations, the next week for apéritifs and accolades," Constanza explained at the entrance of Dash Siebenthrall in "The Bad-Tempered Cavalier," one of the more fulminating chapters of her unabashed autobiography.

a

adamantine

in the figurative sense—the one that captivates the curiosity of Frangipani—*adamantine* means inflexible, unyielding, so hard as to be impenetrable; flinty, firm, unmovable

> "I may be otherwise amok, at loose ends," pontificated Flip Valinthrob, "but on this issue of dressing the dummy à la mode de Schlaffenfuss, I side unflinchingly with Nada Seria: my preference is adamantine for a simple muslin shift over the shameless rustle of silk pajamas."

admonish

to reprove mildly or kindly, but seriously; to warn or exhort by pointing out something forgotten or disregarded; to scold and warn with same breath and with wagging finger

> . . . admonished by her buckled lips
> —Emily Dickinson

adumbrate

to prefigure indistinctly; to foreshadow; to disclose partially or guardedly; to give a sketchy outline of

> I should like to adumbrate for you, dear reader, several of the themes that arabesque their way through these pages: cowboys with lingerie, death and resurrection, abduction and ransom, opera buffa and seriosa, and above all words living beyond their meanings—an abduction of another order, in which you too take place.

4

aficionado

an enthusiast, devotee, fan; a passionate admirer

> Opera aficionados may find the contralto's memoirs puzzling, for she mentions works with twisted titles and alludes to roles she implies she has sung that belong to sopranos.

amanuensis

a taker of dictation or copier of manuscripts; the origin is submissive: the word first denoted a slave of handwriting

> "It's not so much that I want to be your amanuensis as that I want to exhale my cigarette smoke into the air you breathe," wrote one applicant for that position with the moribund contralto. Needless to say, the honor went to an admirer who would not menace her chest, for Constanza Zermattress had a pack of arias and tales yet to sing before she'd consent to expire.

amaranthine

of the amaranth, an unfading flower; eternally beautiful and unfading; everlasting

> The room, which she called her Salon des Refusés, was an oxymoronic mixture of the neglected and the amaranthine, with trashy novels by Strophe Dulac, then first editions, under glass, of such classics as *Handful of Mist* and *The Lapsed Credenza*; ashtrays from the Last Judg-

ment Pinball Machine Motel; mirrors reflecting eternal youth; a Baby Shiraz Persian carpet beneath a baby grand piano; raddled drapes and fatigued fauteuils; the stolen *Fishmonger Taking His Carp Back in a Huff* and *Young Girl Wringing the Neck of Her Mandolin* alongside precious, resplendent Old Masters.

amplitude

greatness of size; fullness, spaciousness, capaciousness, commodiousness, abundance, plenteousness, copiousness

The amplitude of the manor's library was not lost on her; it was *she* who was lost in that voluminous room.

anodyne

something that soothes pain, a source of soothing comfort; as an adjective, capable of soothing or eliminating pain; comforting

"I'm afraid," said the wizard without the slightest soupçon of *Schadenfreude*, "that what is needed here is an anodyne of such prodigious potency that it would flatten the spikes on hairdos for miles around and dulcify the palace guards and court jester out of their livelihoods—and that, too, could pose a threat to the mental balance of our sovereign."

...mirrors reflecting eternal youth...

a

anomalous

abnormal; deviant; deviating from the normal or common order, form, or rule

> . . . and he kissed the already anomalous bride.
> — *The Wretch of Lugubria*

antidote

a medicine or other remedy for counteracting the effects of poison or disease; something that prevents or counteracts injurious or unwanted effects

> "Oh, he's the very antidote to desire!"
> — Congreve, *The Way of the World*

aperçu

a discerning perception, an insight; a hasty glance or quick impression, a glimpse; a summary or synopsis

> You can't base your assessment on a mere aperçu; take this affable rogue off our hands for a week—but please, in another country!

apotheosis

exaltation to divine status, deification; an exalted or glorified example

> She took her grievances to Dark & Rush, Solicitors, on

East of the Sun, West of the Moment Street, in a monstrous office block that is the very apotheosis of the nondescript; even its shadow scintillates with mediocrity and error without trial.

apposite

fitting, suitable, appropriate; strikingly apt or relevant

Her hat, not quite apposite for the solemn occasion, was a little number by Rudi Grotto, the bad boy of headgear and footwear, and looked like Bambi in the Land of Cockaigne—or Brueghel in Disneyland.

approbation

an expression of approval, praise; validation, sanction; official approval, imprimatur

How desperately she needed his all-out approbation to go through with her slightest intent!
— *The Motown Mogul and the Mohairy Princess*

asseverate

to avow earnestly, affirm, proclaim

"Oh! You send shivarees down my spine!" asseverated the satiating satyr's new bride.

aureate

golden in color, gilded; written or spoken in pompous, florid style

> They call him the Poet Aureate, with his golden locks,
> his ornate orations, his poems pulsating with hypersen-
> suosities and Orientalist potpourris (see *The Abduction
> of the Magi* and "The Sedentary Tsatzkeleh," a fable,
> not a poem, about a bedroom-
> eyed hussy and her hookah),
> his brocade bindings
> and frothy palindromes.

avoirdupois

weight or heaviness, especially of a person

> "Is your avoirdupois diminishing beneath that yurt
> of sand-washed silk?"
>
> "No, I haven't really lost weight; I've just consoli-
> dated my resources."

berserk

crazy, mad, out of one's mind; from *berserker*, a Norse warrior who fought with wild and frenzied fury

> Not only was he going ever so imperceptibly berserk, but he was also going it alone.
> — *The Madman and the Mezzotinter*

besom

a broom

> She made a clean sweep of the mess with her trusty dust cloth and tufted besom.

> What a burning, bright besom she rode on her forays through the darkened skies.
> — *The Sorceress, the Famulus, and the Prodigal Daughter*

Bildungsroman

a novel that details the psychological development of the principal character

> *The Man in the Grey Flannel Suite* is a Bildungsroman about Trill Apasaguena, who outgrows the feet of his childhood pajamas and topples the world's markets in several commodities while wearing nothing but a necktie in his grisly penthouse office.

We interrupt this alphabetical free fall for a visit to a bordello.

bordello

a brothel

Jonquil, a vivacious, ratted-haired blonde in high school, had turned into a nebulous, though still wanton, introvert by the time she'd finished with Descartes. Her professor, preoccupied in those days with ethics (and brimming with perspicuous insights, fatuous hindsights, sagacious sound bites), could not take his eyes off her knees during his lectures, and was discomfited with lascivious thoughts. How might he lead her into tenebrous chambers with a thousand pillows and drifting, silken light beams, then expose his tendentious intentions? He would propose a preposterous night under the town and throw off his donnish gown! The truth is, Jonquil was way ahead of him on this one, and was already setting up on her own! What had become of the gregarious wench of old, with her nail polishes, raucous laughter, flashing eyes? Quoting Diderot, "My ideas are my trollops," she opened a brothel of platonic love where fetching notions, scantily clad and fatally attractive, drove many a young man out of his mind and into business, pre-med, or law.

fatuous
> foolish — vacuously and smugly so

gregarious
> sociable, reveling in the company of others

lascivious
> lusty, lewd, or exciting sexual desires in others

nebulous
> cloudy, misty, hazy; vague, without definite form or limits

perspicuous
> clearly expressed, presented; easy to comprehend

preposterous
> outrageous, absurd; flying in the face of nature or reason

raucous
> making harsh throaty sounds, perhaps like a crow

sagacious
> showing sound judgment and discernment; wise

tendentious
> marked by a strong implicit point of view; written or spo-
> ken to promote some cause; biased

tenebrous
> dark, gloomy, in shadows

vivacious
> lively, animated

b

bravura

showy manner, daring display; brilliant performance; a florid musical passage or piece demanding of the performer great spirit and skill

"I was as notorious for my bedroom eyes and bedtime bravura as I was celebrated for my coloratura," continued Constanza over antipasto alfresco,* recalling an interlude in Duque de Caxias during a season in Rio de Janeiro.

brouhaha

uproar, hubbub, ruckus

The imputations were all shorter than two feet tall, but their brouhaha went over our heads.

cabriole

a leg of a table or chair that curves outward and then tapers in and down to a clawlike foot grasping a ball (which is usually stationary); from French, *caper:* a balletic leap with one leg extended and then the feet are struck quickly together

After slamming her fabled dresser drawer, Charmiane was resoundingly floored by the chance encounter of her heel with the claw of a cabriole.

---

* alfresco: outdoors, in the open air

cache

a hiding place, especially in the ground, for ammunition, food, or treasure; anything so hidden

> We're stashing these pearls that were his eyes in a little cache on the other island.

cachinnate

to laugh loudly, immoderately, resoundingly, convulsively

> The truckling tone of his marriage proposal left her flailing and cachinnating helplessly and wondering what he'd actually meant.

callipygian

having beautifully proportioned buttocks

> At the Symposium on Literary Pulchritude, Francis Rawsthorne defended his assertion that Roubaud's beautiful heroine with the not so euphonious name is a paragon of callipygian perfection.

calumniate

to slander; to say knowingly malicious falsehoods about

> "Don't calumniate me like that! It just makes me wish I'd done something *really* bad."
> > —*The Duchess of Malfatti*

castigate

to inflict severe punishment; to severely criticize, rebuke, berate, chastise

> She hurled us into a backlit corner and proceeded to castigate us sanctimoniously and soft-soap us purple-prosaically.
>
> — *The Velveteen Rabble*

catalepsy

a condition of muscular rigidity and lack of response to external stimuli, with the limbs remaining in whatever position they are placed

> Playing captive audience was no longer her cup of tea after her long session, with her long legs, at the Eagle Café, where a perfect stranger had harangued her into a catalepsy of enthralled listening and left her in a senseless (but enlightened, he thought) heap (the legs folded quite easily: it runs in the family, as this line-up of her uncles attests).

cellar door

> The word for "torch" is the most beautiful in French, *chalumeau*, a close rival to Edgar Allan Poe's proposal for the most beautiful sound in English, *cellar door.*
>
> — Edmund White, *Our Paris*

Playing captive audience was no longer her cup of tea after her long session, with her long legs, at the Eagle Café, where a perfect stranger had harangued her into a catalepsy of enthralled listening and left her in a senseless (but enlightened, he thought) heap (the legs folded quite easily: it runs in the family, as this line-up of her uncles attests).

charivari, also shivaree

noisy mock serenade to newlyweds, often with banging pots and pans; from a French word related to headache, the natural upshot of this nuptial clamor

> Emanating from the Palaz of Hoon was a charivari of shiny woks and broken hearts.

> Along with champagne, condoms, and maids on tiptoe, the Honeymoon Hotel offered, to second-marriage guests, a shivaree of nightingales and crows.

chasmophile

a lover and seeker-out of nooks and crannies

> You tell that chasmophile she's wanted here in the spotlight, on the double, and if she comes out clutching her shadow in a full-frontal embrace, we'll toss her into the troupe of supernumerary spear holders, and that recalcitrant showoff can huddle in her armor to her heart's content, where even the accolades won't bite her!

chthonic

of or pertaining to the underworld and its deities and spirits; dark, primitive, mysterious, infernal

> "I've had my tussles with chthonic creatures, I've had my bouts with the bottle, I've wrestled with consciences not shaped like my own, and now all I want is a lipstick

that will hold its own with lots of kissers, a bed to muscle my bones," declared Angie Canasta in her last interview with Rafael Todos los Muertos.

cicerone

a guide who conducts sightseers

Walls, walkways, our very own feet obscured by the famous Adriatic fog, the *nebbia*, we clung to the shirttails of our cicerone, a proud, patient man with polished side whiskers who knew Venice like the back of his mother's hairbrush and led us unflinchingly through echoing passages and vacant vias, over sighing bridges, past loggias and lions as silent as stone in the unreflected city.

claque

a group of hired applauders or voluntary truly fawning admirers

The queen was most certainly *not* amused by the diva's drunken pantomime, and her claque was mortified.

cognoscente, cognoscenti (plural)

persons with superior knowledge and understanding of a particular field, especially in the fine arts, literature, and fashion

The gathering was indeed formidable: a collection of idiot savants holding forth on their specialties while the cognoscenti of contemporary literature skulked off to powder their notions or cowered on couches and passed out on porches among their muted allusions.

coiffeur

hairdresser, *artiste* of the hair, who creates coiffures

> My coiffeur calls it his "Fantasy in F-sharp minor," and my husband says it's "Goldilocks at the Moulin Rouge," although I'm not quite sure what the latter means — curls atumble from the cancan, in the absinthe of three bears?

compunction

pang of doubt or guilt, foreshadowing (or foreshadowed by) wrongdoing; a relative of a *qualm*

> Yea, though I stray occasionally from the path of righteousness without compunction, I shall sidle up to no evil or suspicious characters, nor shall I live more than occasionally in a world of make-believe.

compunctious

uneasy or scrupulous about the fitness or propriety of an act or a thing; feeling guilt or remorse

> The day, a compunctious Sunday after a week of riots and blizzards, had been part jewel, part mud.

concatenation

the outcome of concatenating, of course!—that is, connecting, linking in a chain or series

You ask how I like the quotes from José Lezama Lima. Great! That's my kind of fun. "The lights made their rounds on laughing arrows like baby goats." What a splendid human phenomenon is metaphor! That's the way God thinks. The whole cosmos as a concatenation of parts rubbing together into life, one big, happy universal figure of speech. They spoke metaphor in the Garden until one day Adam framed a proposition in prose and Eve said "Yes," and that was that. But they took a little metaphor with them when they slid down the slope toward Moses, and not even Martin Luther succeeded in rinsing it away.

—Paul Aaen Gordon

What a face to come home to!
Twinkling, mocking, and contrite.

concupiscence

sexual desire, lust, lasciviousness

> Concupiscence bridges many a lap.
> —*The Seventy Carnal Synonyms*

> . . . never knowing whose voice she's hearing, confusing the *monde* and the mind, mistaking even the concupiscent lurchings of her own body for Popean acrobatics.

conniption

a fit of hysterical excitement or anger; *conniption* is a genuinely American expression of nevertheless uncertain provenance

> "Now don't you go blowing up this minor contretemps into a Dostoyevskian conniption," Yolanta pleaded with the rhinestone cowboy whose silk teddy had gotten tattered in a barroom brawl.

consanguine, consanguineous

of the same lineage, descent, or origin; having a common ancestor

> Consanguine we may be, regrettable cousin, but our politics render us fisticuffs company at these tables of holiday bubbles and grease.

contrite

penitent; feeling regret and sorrow for one's own actions; guilty, remorseful

> What a face to come home to! Twinkling, mocking, and contrite.

cortege

a train of attendants, as of a potentate; a retinue; a funeral procession

> She stood in the receiving line as the cortege shuffled by, pumping her arm with unctuous good wishes and sniffing her corsage.

> The cortege seemed to have hit a snag as it entered the cemetery; several calèches buckled, and a white mare nipped a chip off the stranded bier.

coruscation

a gleam, glint, sparkle, glitter

> Before getting the sack for making a crack about "Molotovian cocktail hours," the captain's recreation and refection officer vouchsafed to the refugees from Bosoxia shipboard romance against nacreous nightscapes, which included pelagic acrobats amidst phosphorescent coruscations glancing off the surface of the sea.

coterie

a small, sometimes select group of persons who often meet, go about together, or otherwise associate

> Shambling after the dissipated diva through the splattered spa town of Schaden Baden was a coterie of opera addicts in low spirits and sharkskin tights—desperate for the sonorous fix that would come much later that evening.

coup de grâce

a death blow; a finishing stroke or decisive event

> Swooping in for the coup de grâce with an "Et tu, Brutus?" was an avenging angel who did a bit of Shakespearean acting and mercenary soul-snatching on the side, and sometimes muffed his lines.

credenza

a buffet or sideboard; originally referred to the place, a cautionary zone, where food was set out for servants to taste before serving it, to verify that nothing was poisoned; the word, in Italian, means trust

> "Help yourselves to the panettone and frangipane on the credenza," coaxed their hostess, winking at the footman on the ottoman, where once her Doberman had bared his draconian soul and was tricked out in furbelows as punishment.
>
> —*The Espresso Murders*

crepuscular

of or like twilight

> Noah Webster's last words, "The room is growing crepuscular," put the old codger before us in a fine light. Pedantically genteel, they were worthy of the schoolmaster whose *A Grammatical Institute of the English Language . . .* had sold in millions—and is still in print—and whose *An American Dictionary of the English*

Language was the Republic's absolute arbiter of spelling and usage. In one of its hefty volumes his grieving but puzzled family found the meaning of "crepuscular."

—Guy Davenport

cupidity

excessive desire, especially for material wealth; avarice

Cupidity held sway over the best minds of the country; the abacus had ousted the lorgnette.

—*The Man in the Grey Flannel Suite*

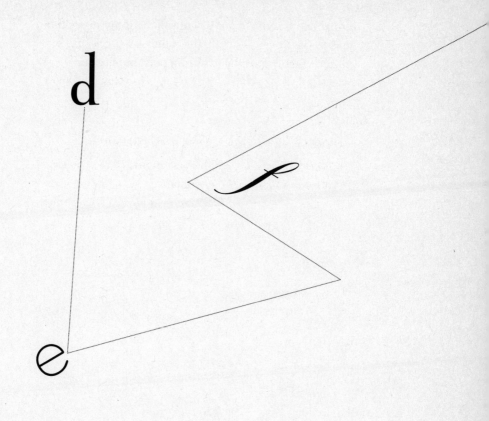

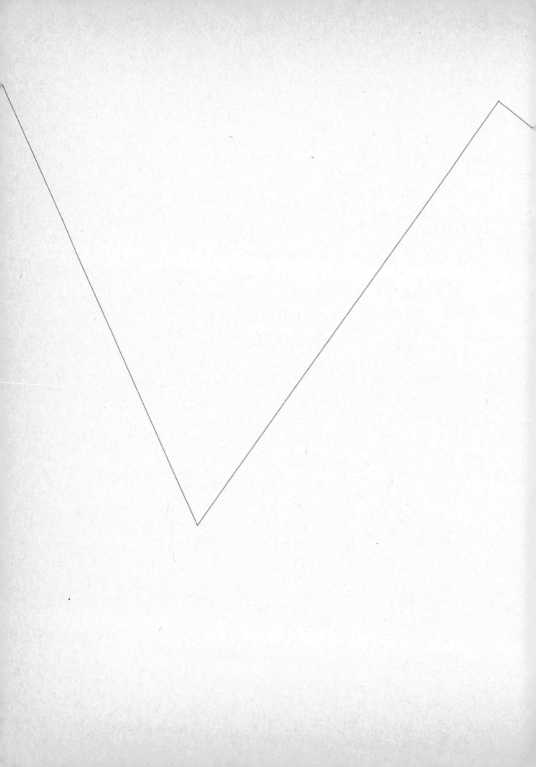

décharné

emaciated, lean, attenuated, skeletal; literally, without flesh

> She wore the décharné look that sometimes haunted her after she'd repelled the advances of many tall dark chocolate mousses and swallowed the frogs in the footman's eyes.

décolletage

a low neckline, especially of a woman's dress, loudly announcing the bust

> The cups of her bra runneth not exactly over, but this isn't the era of décolletage.

déjà vu

a feeling or illusion that one has previously experienced what is happening now, which is happening for the first time

> . . . and then this creepy sense of déjà vu insinuated

itself among all those present, giving them in one shared swoon some reason for being together, when they'd entered the room as total strangers twenty minutes earlier.

— *The Velveteen Rabble*

demure

modest and reserved in manner or behavior; affectedly shy and modest—one might even say coy

> Nibbling at the circumference of the conversation, she demurely ushered the borage, rampion, and nasturtiums to her salad plate's edge and munched pensively on a *cochon de lait.**

denizen

an inhabitant, a resident; a habitué: one who regularly frequents a place

> Those conniving denizens of the dappled underworld are in cahoots with the Angel Food League.

depravity

moral corruption or degradation, the upshot of debauchery

> Beguilingly delectable—horrifically rich—the cloying pastry cart of her depravity was indeed a dubious treat.

* suckling pig

despondency

low spirits brought on by loss of hope, courage, or confidence; despair

> Oh, 'tis the very rapture of despondency upon me! My handkerchief and I must retire to my boudoir at once!
>
> *—The Wretch of Lugubria*

desultory

moving, jumping from one thing to the next; disconnected; random, haphazard

> . . . so we got the machinery in motion for a perfectly desultory evening of carnal non sequiturs.

diatribe

a bitter, abusive denunciation; a vituperative tongue-lashing

> She stood there, a diatribe in underwear, while the cowboys sang a lullaby soft as satin, without a trace of lace.
>
> *—from Yolanta's notes on Out West lingerie*

diffidence

timidity, shyness, self-deprecating reluctance to assert one's rights or wishes; a lack of self-confidence

> Often these malevolent winds from Trajikistan bring euphoria, buoyancy, even manic surges of energy and diffidence; but then the horrific second phase sets in,

d

and frenzied acts of impertinence and aggression tumble from one soul to another, till even the most sanctimonious citizen has beheld the loud hound of darkness thrashing about in his home.

disconsolate

hopelessly sad; very dejected indeed; cheerless or gloomy

> We took our cares down to the corner and threw darts at a darkened eyeball for an hour in a disconsolate pub.

> How straight to his heart went her guttersnipe allure— her sweet and disconsolate temperament, her get-ups of opossum fur.

divagation

wandering, straying, going astray; digressing in speech

> The ventriloquist's divagations took a turn south, with a lexical jambalaya and an anecdote about his great-aunt Foxie Belle Bloom catching crawdads in the bayou with her torch songs and ululations and her Blond Assassin lacquered nails (from the Emily Dickinson cosmetics collection).

divertissement

a brief performance, often a ballet which comes as an interlude in an opera or play; more generally, an entertainment or amusement

> Pleading a migraine of the moment, a meeting on the morrow, the Duchess Ilona excused herself from the

Often these malevolent winds from Trajikistan bring euphoria, buoyancy, even manic surges of energy and diffidence; but then the horrific second phase sets in, and frenzied acts of impertinence and aggression tumble from one soul to another, till even the most sanctimonious citizen has beheld the loud hound of darkness thrashing about in his home.

d

Dolce far niente *is also one of the most popular
desserts at Café Frangipane, and comes with
complimentary silk pajamas, a tumulus of cushions, a troupe of untroubled succubi and incubi
to see you to your door.*

divertissement she'd rumpled her hair and undressed for — "Perturbation for Pianoforte and Night Visitors" — and staggered out to the electric esplanade for a gulp of chilled and chastening air.

dolce far niente

pleasant inactivity; literally, sweet to do nothing

Taking leave of their usual antediluvian roustabouting, the mastodons gave themselves over to the *dolce far niente* of a faunal afternoon.

Dolce far niente is also one of the most popular desserts at Café Frangipane, and comes with complimentary silk pajamas, a tumulus of cushions, a troupe of untroubled succubi and incubi to see you to your door.

Doppelgänger

a double, in literature or real life, and a popular figure in nine-teenth-century literature, haunting various protagonists and often driving them mad

It is my Doppelgänger who is eating my bear claw and has been duplicating our efforts.

dossier

a collection of papers giving detailed information about a particular person or subject

We've worked up this dossier on Monsieur Joubert Plume, who turns out to have spent several years in the water traffic of Azuriko—posing as a robber.

doyenne

a woman who is the eldest or senior member of a group

> Strophe Dulac, the undisputed doyenne of bodice-ripping metafiction, has written metacriticisms for *Licking the Beast* and a riot of novelettas such as *The Duchess of Malfatti* and *Creepy Suzette.*

draconian

unusually harsh or severe, as of policy, punishment, or law

> Retribution in Azuriko was positively draconian for those guilty of platitudinous expression: drug traffickers got off easy compared with citizens who were judged to have too prodigally laced their conversations with clichés and chosen-with-carelessness idioms.

dulcify

Can't you imagine from *dolce far niente* that *dulcify* also aims for pleasure? It means to sweeten, soften, soothe, mollify, make gentle, and it will happen in Café Frangipane when you reach for your refections.

effrontery

shameless or impudent boldness; candid, brazen audacity; insolence, impudence, chutzpah with no apologies

> Jonquil, twice expelled from Amplochacha University

for compulsive effrontery, decided to make her way in the world without a degree and swiftly apprenticed herself to the éminence grise of Louvelandia, a quixotic cartographer.

éminence grise

once upon a time, the power behind the throne; more often these days, the guy calling the shots in the shadows: a powerful adviser or decision-maker who operates secretly or unofficially; literally, a grey eminence

ensellure

the concave curve formed by the spine; in woman, the lumbar incurvation

So rapturous over the dorsal view of his new mannequin was Gregor Schlaffenfuss that he created an audacious line of backless gowns and gadabouts inspired by her callipygian charms and her enigmatic ensellure.

ersatz

artificial, synthetic, imitation, simulated, fake

We had a mock turtle soup followed by an ersatz snail soufflé, and that was but the beginning of a soirée where nothing was what it seemed.

e

esplanade

a flat, open expanse of pavement or grass, especially one inviting promenades along a shore or in a cityscape, such as the City of Light's Esplanade des Invalides

> The esplanade was pullulating with hookers and loners, dope fiends and dowagers, sightseers abandoned by their cicerones.

evince

to show clearly, make manifest; to reveal the possession of a quality, trait, proclivity

> Her Doppelgänger evinced no objection or astonishment when abandoned in the tow-away zone.

exhort

to urge by strong admonition; to make an urgent appeal; to cheer on vociferously

> And he nuzzled my pulse points all cheap cologne yeah and he cuffed me sweetly about the room and yeah I exhorted him yeah oh yeah.
>
> —*Pierrot and the Whiplash*

expurgate

to remove juicy, vulgar, obscene, or otherwise offensive, even erroneous, material from a book prior to publication

> We expurgated prudishly all the manuscripts that fell into our hands and combined the offensive segments into a bold new work.

We expurgated prudishly all the manuscripts that fell into our hands and combined the offensive segments into a bold new work.

e

extirpate

to uproot, pull out; to utterly destroy, exterminate; to remove by surgery

> You hold 'im down and shut his mouth while I extirpate these here tenacious boots and give the socks to Cerberus.
>
> —from the "Socks and Bondage" scene of *Cowboys and Lingerie*

famulus

a medieval sorcerer's or scholar's apprentice

> The *Walpurgisnacht* revelers included a talcum-powdered, timorous banshee; a white witch strapped to an ergonomic plowshare; an enchanted donkey with chattering teeth; and a famulus looking very out of sorts in oversized madras shorts.

fantoccini

puppets whose animation comes from mechanical means; a play or puppet show in which they are the stars. Looking for origins, we find children, from the diminutive *fante*, child, of *infante*. A puppet master does sometimes think of the puppets as his children, after all.

Commedia dell'Arte Scenario

Cutting a woozy swath, Arlecchino enters and traces suggestive arabesques in the air ambidextrously. Ursalina stomps out like 6.4 on the Richter scale. Alarmed, Pantalone skids onto the stage with his *fantoccini* in fur coats. Burattino gives him a big smack and hastens to demystify Goldonio's departure by producing the compromising fan, by now battered to splinters and silken tatters. The puppets squeak "Ciao!" but Pantalone says, "Not yet, my angelini," and brings out his concertina, at which they tenderly cover each other's ears and settle down for a painful *sinfonia disconcertante*. Colombina prances in, pushing a pram and munching a panettone. Out of the pram pops Petrouchka with some guidelines for *perestroika*. All hie their colorful bodies and language to a caffè on the corner and knock back a few espressos till the train to Rome arrives and they can settle down to some very serious business: stealing wallets and laptops. White-collar crimes are their favorites.

f

*All hie their colorful bodies and language
to a caffe on the corner and knock back a
few espressos till the train to Rome arrives
and they can settle down to some very serious business: stealing wallets and laptops.
White-collar crimes are their favorites.*

feckless

lacking purpose or vitality; feeble, ineffective; careless, irresponsible; from Scottish, *feck*, for efficacy, short for *effect + less*

> As the nuptial repast careened off course, the bride abashed the feckless groom and turned him over to her uncle.

felonious

criminal, miscreant, malfeasant, naughty; having the nature of a felony

> "I could find little harmony, though, in the happiness that fluttered about my heart like a felonious magpie," Constanza equivocated about her affair with a keyed-up basso profundo.

fermata

in music, the prolongation of a note, chord, tone, or rest beyond its indicated time value

> I once flirted for thirty seconds with Too-Too LaBlanca, but at about the twenty-third second I said to myself, "This is ridiculous. *Everybody* flirts with Too-Too LaBlanca," and quickly diminuendoed to an eternal fermata.
>
> —Harvey Sachs

flamingo

From Portuguese and Spanish, originally applied to Flemish people, who were known to have ruddy complexions. But the color attached to the bird flamingo for its flaming appearance. (If you wish to meet a colorful character from Flanders and discover why you are reading this book, then flip ahead to the penultimate entry, where James Ensor delivers the reason.)

A flamingo had followed Jonquil home and fallen in love with her goosenecked lamp.

flummery

utter nonsense, figuratively; oatmeal or blancmange, literally

Knock off the flummery and get on with the ax-grindery.

formication

a tactile hallucination involving the sensation that things are crawling on or under one's skin

Guests checked into the Last Judgment Pinball Machine Motel for all manner of diversion and debauchery—from formication to Spin the Bottle, bondage to boundless gratification, driving hard bargains in the bathtub or frangipanicking in their pajamas, writing billets-doux to their congressmen, and tossing kisses out the windows to charmless passersby.

fractious

unruly, refractory; quick to anger, fume, and quarrel

> "I feel quite wet with rage!" spluttered the fractious contralto, storming off the stage.

frangible

breakable, fragile

> "I'm a connoisseur of anything frangible, my dear — tsatskelehs, bone china, incidental music, yearning hearts."
>
> — *Moxie in Paramatta*

fraught

filled or charged with something; accompanied; fully laden or provided

> . . . a train fraught with standing ribs only, eyes of round, briskets, and veal
> — Huis van Scudder, *The Abattoir of Kasteel Beverweert*

> . . . a look fraught with meanings not quite clear, intentions asqueak with fond hopes
> — *The Girl with the Golden Eyesore*

fripperous

from *frippery*, which is gaudy, ostentatious finery and other superficial forms of display

> "Ah, bedraggled and tucked in at last! Nothing fripperous about a set of clean sheets!"
>
> — *Menace in Venice*

froufrou, also frou-frou

fussy, showy, frivolous dress or ornamentation; from the sound
of rustling silk

> The chintz curtains look like a nightmare my great-aunt
> Foxy Belle Bloom might have had when her sloe gin ran
> out, and the threadbare carpet, a nice spartan touch,
> hardly makes up for the knee-deep froufrou in your
> phone booth, which you must have dragged in from a
> brothel during the Prussian siege of Paris when Victor
> Hugo was eating rats.
> — Jusko Bou Trompe, at Hotel Crillon Sans Ascenseur

fulgurant

flashing like lightning; dazzlingly bright

> After this fulgurant muck has cooled to the temperature
> of an idle hand, remove to a tenebrous corner and serve
> on a bed of steaming peccadilloes.

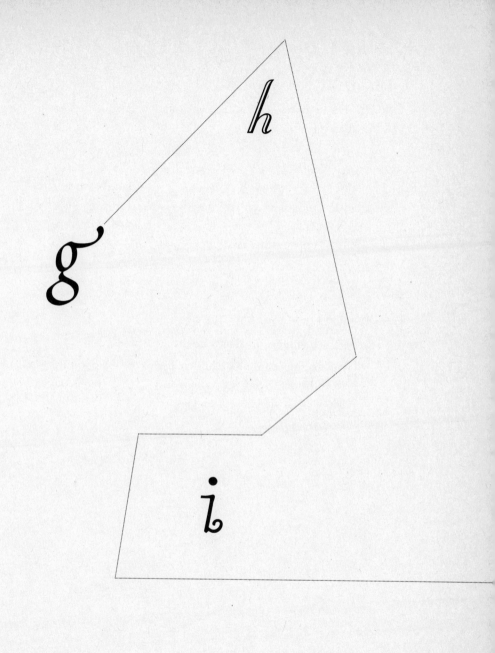

galoot, also galloot

a clumsy, awkward, uncouth person

> In an address delivered to a pack of gamins now painfully grown into adolescents, Strophe Dulac solaced them with a few anecdotes from her own teenage bewilderments and with this observation from the decades since: "We are all galoots at one time or another; *life* is the self-conscious, awkward phase, not this or that decade within it."

gambado

a leaping or gamboling movement, probably resembling the capers James Boswell was advised by his doctor to cut about his room to lighten his melancholia

> The guys performed their gambadoes, heaved the dumbbells, and retired to the Turkish baths.

genius loci

the spirit or character of a place; originally associated with ancient Rome: it was believed that every place (house, institution) has a guardian spirit

Dear Loona,

Just a quick postcard (those are some of the famous cascades of Azuriko, which by now we've left far behind — although not before tossing one of my earrings into the one called Das Knaben Wunderhorn to ensure a musically talented child: local tradition, and the counsels of my godmother Constanza) to say that rather than dallying our honeymoon away in Trajikistan (you were dead right about the genius loci there), we betook ourselves to the next country west and are now (after difficulties at the border) amusing ourselves quite bestially in Lavukistan (good thing we got our visas for here, too; that "just in case" mentality has always been my saving grace) and will be home in twenty days. As for Trajikistan, there was a conference on labyrinths at the Hotel Flambeau, and they'd brought in an architect from Hotel Mostar in Paris to completely redo the corridors. Talk about genius loci! I divined the presence of the minotaur in the depths of the hotel—the pantry, I suppose, wolfing down continental breakfasts (inapt verb, but too late now) and nuzzling the scullery maids hopelessly in his thrall.

Bye for now, thanks for the poltergeist—such an original gift, and I wish we'd brought it with us, as it might have come to our assistance in Trajikistan.

Love, and laku noć,

Laurinda

Talk about genius loci! I divined the presence of the minotaur in the depths of the hotel—the pantry, I suppose, wolfing down continental breakfasts (inapt verb, but too late now) and nuzzling the scullery maids hopelessly in his thrall.

g

*. . . those are some of the famous cascades
of Azuriko, which by now we've
left far behind . . .*

gossamer

and the Angelic Saxophone

This is a fragment of the introduction that ambled off to another page—or did it fly on wings of gossamer?—to become more than a divertissement at the heart of this book, for Anglo-Saxon and Old Norse words are at the very heart of our language, and form the matrix of this book too: every sentence is animated by them and could not get far without them. *Gossamer*, to set this off on the proper feet (webbed ones), comes from some antique language for "goose summer," or so one etymology affirms.

What impelled, or imperiled, me into graduate school years ago, besides a desire to prolong my childhood, was Chaucer's company in the late night hours of a New Mexico winter, intimations of sounds that ran riot in Old and Middle English and still give our language much of its punch and precision, its music, its xylophonic backbone, its trudging and lilting gait. No matter that the first week on campus I followed a poet carrying a soft old lamp down a basement corridor (no, he did not look like a white rabbit) and got sidetracked—or abducted—into twentieth-century poetry, including my own. I've come back to the fourteenth century in my own sweet time (and indeed we never really parted), finding its voice as alluring as ever, especially after several winters in Paris, where there are no verbs to convey in one happy capsule of syllables the idea of tottering, staggering, shambling, shuffling, or any other way most of us get around. So I sashayed home. Never mind for the moment that the great transformations in Middle English, handed down to us, came through the Norman Conquest, the influence of French and its Latin ancestry, pouring into the Anglo-Saxon pool.

Is it something about winter solstices and dimming lights that evokes these stark and glittering sounds? Each year at this time they seem to surge and renew their force. Several days wrapped up in my blankets and dictionaries here confirm what I suspected: most of the words that are the daily bread of our mumbled mouthfuls, that are the rhythms and textures I love rubbing against Latinate vocables in English (well, yes, mellifluous ones like *imbroglio, bravado, marzipan, taffeta, langouste,* and *lagniappe*), come from those Anglo-Saxons and Vikings I was after before taking my Incomplete in *The Romance of the Rose* and *Sir Gawain and the Green Knight,* and letting someone else play the Wife of Bath, so I could have nervous breakdowns and write poetry instead.

Tearing through *Webster's* and *The American Heritage Dictionary* in my oubliette, I nearly always find the Middle English or Old English origin I hotly pursue, although some words I was certain were Nordic or Anglo-Saxon prove to be imitative, like *clanking,* or Middle Dutch, like *cookie. Clanking* shouldn't be a surprise: many of the Old English verbal ancestors are onomatopoetic—one reason they so impellingly call to me, are so readily, without explanation, understood. *Crisp* comes into Old English from Latin—a language I studied at fourteen with a cherubic monk manqué who kindly passed me in physics too, although I sat through those classes beneath Mr. Sponar's avuncular very nose openly reading trash like *Gone with the Wind* and wishing to be as ravishingly troublesome as Scarlett O'Hara while Rhett Butler pulled my ringlets and carried me up the stairs.

One of the beauties of these words is that they need no definition: they've been with us so long they're in our bones and blood, they played with our mouths when we first started speaking — in the history of the language, in our individual infancies, our own lone babyhoods. Even the abstract nouns seem palpable; we can almost handle them as physically as we experience them: hope fear love time shame hunger wrath.

On the following two pages are a few handfuls of sounds that fell out of the angelic saxophone and tumbled into the twentieth century to enliven its prose, our every utterance, to hound us from birth and beyond death. Just get a load of the onomatopoeia gushing, gnashing, flitting, and flashing through these words!

g

aghast drizzle froth* gap*

amaze drowsy forgive gather

asunder eerie foam ghost

awful elf, elfin flutter gleam

awkward ember fluster* glide

bleak fey flotilla* glint‡

blunder* fling† float glisten

bluster* flit* glitter

brazen gloaming

bustle* gloom

cake* glove*

clack glow*

clamber grim

clap grisly

clasp groan

clumsy ice

crawl kiss

craze† lap

creep lark

crumble *dawn* leer

cunning light

darling lissome

dawn lope*

daze lout

dazzle lurk†

deep lust

doom mist

door mood

---

murk   ruthless   sky   snow

pout   scruffy†   slay   spark

prance   shadow   sleep   sprawl

rainbow   shame   slog

rather   shatter   slut§

moon   roar   shy   smack

motley   ruffle*   skip*   smoke

mug†   rugged†   skulk†   snag*

sky

stagger   swarthy   tumble

star   swoop   twinkle

stark   tatter   wag*

startle   thrall*   waif*   woe

sultry   thrill   wander   wolf

throttle   wanton   wonder

thrum*   whirl*   wrath

thrust*   wit*   wretch

thunder*   wizard   yammer

* Old Norse   † Scandinavian   ‡ Danish, Swedish   § Norwegian

g

My oral fixation on our earliest Englishes has led to many trysts in the stacks, sucking suffixes and Ur-sprachen, tasting silver syllables and kisses. As I was flailing about on the floor there one day, my fluttered hand chanced to grab an odd volume, on a nether shelf, of almost Middle English literature consisting of two distinct works, *Gossamer and the Green Light* and *The Churl*, both dubiously attributed to the same author literary history has dubbed the *Churl* Poet. I have applied to the Vast Monthrock Foundation for a grant to look further into the *Gossamer* text and establish its author as female. *The Churl* is surely by the *Churl* Poet, but *Gossamer* must have been written by a girl poet who was writing, avant-guardedly, in prose, and I'm burning with certainty that the green light will prove me right, as I alone can read by it. I have rendered some fragments into modern English for the delectation of contempo readers, and here quote them in order to expose some of our current everyday words to the light of Gossamer's lamp.

THIS WAS A TIME when people were still known by their footsteps and beggars were rewarded for their trouble. A time when manners mattered twice as much as madness and half as much as magic . . .

A GREAT GNASHING of TEETH and POPPING of KNUCKLES FOLLOWED and MANY HARD FEELINGS got thwacked about, and MANY WINGS were BRUISED.

Now don't you worry—THINGS are skittering along toward the BRINK of the abyss, and NOTHING you or I might do will alter their AWFUL course.

We stretched our imaginations across the chasm of our doubts and proceeded with QUAKING BELIEF.

There was ONCE a MAN who LIVED in a castle surrounded by a MOAN.

"*A long* time *is little to me,*" *he answered* sadly,
"*but* forever *is* nothing."

I'm WAITING for him to START DAZZLING these cadavers.

"A long TIME is little to me," he answered
SADLY, "but FOREVER is NOTHING."

And so, from these GHASTLY ruminations
we turned to more CHEERFUL topics.

She SWUNG SHUT the DOOR of her SMILE of GREETING,
SLAYING the DARK with her piercing SHRIEKS.

Oh, I don't know about that MOUTH of
hers. SOMETIMES it seems like a gimmick.

SPRING was trilling outside the WINDOW. GOS-
SAMER RAISED her NOSE from the GRINDSTONE
of her NEEDLEWORK and SNIFFED the air.
SOMETHING was TWITTERING inside her, too,
HEAVING her BOSOM and LIFTING her spirits,
which had been so LOW of LATE.

I want you to DRAG me HOME with you
by the ROOTS of my own MEANINGS.

She BROKE the silence engulfing them
with an audible hush and TINGLE.

g

Pleased to make your ᴅᴇᴇᴘ acquaintance.

Your bedroom eyes are ᴛᴡɪɴᴋʟɪɴɢ.

There's no ʟᴜsᴛ ʟᴏsᴛ between us.

And he kept on ʙᴇsᴍɪʀᴄʜɪɴɢ me
although I ʙᴇsᴇᴇᴄʜᴇᴅ him to stop.

Is this going to put a ᴡᴏɴᴅᴇʀꜰᴜʟ
sᴍᴜᴅɢᴇ ꜰᴏʀᴇᴠᴇʀ upon my ɴᴀᴍᴇ?

She sɴᴀɢɢᴇᴅ the ᴛɪᴘ of her ɢʟᴏᴠᴇ's
index ꜰɪɴɢᴇʀ on a sᴘᴏᴋᴇ of her umbrella.
A ᴘᴀᴛᴄʜ of her ᴡɪɴɢ began to ɪᴛᴄʜ.*

My big sᴘʀᴀᴡʟɪɴɢ feet and sɴᴀʀʟᴇᴅ hair wallflowered me.

She ɢᴀᴛʜᴇʀᴇᴅ herself into an anxious horde and
went ꜰʟɪᴛᴛɪɴɢ along the ʀᴏᴀᴅ of her misfortune.

* This creature is one of the Angels of Saxony, I believe.

halcyon

tranquil, calm, peaceful; golden with quality or prosperity

"Ah, but our nostrils did not widen in pleasure then, nor did life caress us and leave us tingling: our halcyon days lay around another twenty corners," dissimulated the contralto to her amanuensis as they braced themselves for another divagation in the composition of her memoirs.

haptic

of or relating to the sense of touch

"I simply *cannot* converse without a bit of haptic stimulation and reassurance," Jonquil stated to the wizard she worked for, narrowing the gap between their two noses and four hands. But do you suppose he yelled, "Tactile harassment!" at her invasion of his senses? Not at all! He was too agog* before this terra incognita that was drawing closer and finding its way to him, and his maps could just get lost.

hauteur

perceptible in both bearing and attitude, *hauteur* is arrogance and haughtiness, a sort of imperious *noli me tangere*, dignity ad absurdum

He was sometimes seized with a wild urge to let down

---

* agog: in a state of keen anticipation, highly excited, astir; agape with wonder; from Old French, *en gogues*, in merriments

h

his hauteur and tear off his pinstripes and roll in a bed
of buttercups and camisoles.
*[This is one of Yolanta's in flagrante delicto snapshots men-
tioned in her* obstreperous *postcard.]*

hirsute

hairy, hairy all over, shaggy

> He showed up in his broken English tweeds—a shabby
> cacophony of hirsute designs.

hubris

arrogance, excessive pride or self-confidence; just the sort of
trait to emphasize when a protagonist is headed for a downfall,
as in many Greek tragedies

> *Adipose Rex*, a modern drama with ancient Greek over-
> tones, is about a king whose hubris vis-à-vis his heart
> and his tragic proclivity for tiropitas, pastitsio, and
> baklava bring on his comeuppance coronary.

ignominious

characterized by shame or disgrace, or deserving them; despica-
ble, degrading, debasing

> Crouching ignominiously amidst the dustballs was their
> disobedient whelp, Nestor Telemachus, readying his
> taut young musculature for an undaunted rebound into
> the hushes and smoke.

imminent

about to occur; impending, approaching, nigh

> Victory was imminent: the final rout would be a piece of cake.

imprecation

a curse; the act of invoking evil upon

> Perturbations running high, they would adjourn for naps in the muddle of most afternoons, fervid dreams and imprecations shouting through their pillows while they snoozed on, baby-faced and becalmed.

imputation

a charge or an accusation of fault or responsibility; attribution, arrogation

> The dreaded imputation arrived, turning our triumphs to dishonor and our gloating to dismay.

inamorata

female sweetheart, lover

> Trinculo's wife, or *sposa*, sent her *sposo*'s inamorata a fistful of spatulas and stilettos in a bouquet of bella-donna.
>
> —*La Inclemenza di Signora Rastito*

ineluctable

inevitable, unavoidable, not about to be escaped

> "My heart was fibrillating like crazy as he whispered, 'Your voice is more than mere enchantment: it's the key to an ineluctable terror menacing an insouciant waif,'" reminisced Constanza, transported to an earlier bedroom furnished with a besotted fan.

ineptitude

incompetence, awkwardness, gaucherie, unseemliness

> I was beside myself with ineptitude, and I felt so ashamed I just wanted to go home and behave myself.

in extremis

at the point of death; in grave or extreme circumstances

> "Are we talking in extremis here, or is this just a social call?" the baba asked the Grim Reaper, who appeared quite suddenly on her TV screen and beckoned her with his scythe toward the cinerary urn she had intended for Nestor Telemachus.

ingenuous

innocent, inexperienced, naive, artless; lacking sophistication and worldliness

Amanda grabbed the mike, stepped out of the spotlight, and snorted an ingenuous aria about clover and honey and crack.

inimical

adverse; injurious or harmful in effect; unfriendly, hostile

The acoustics here are inimical to cozy chats: let's go to Café Frangipane and slip into some susurrant silk pajamas.

innocuous

harmless, innocent, insipid; not likely to offend or incense

The telltale epistle she shredded into innocuous scraps; the flames consumed those fateful phrases that, even as they cindered and expired, scorched her nostrils and twiddled her breasts.

insouciance

a carefree indifference; blithe lack of concern; nonchalance, *désinvolture*

While your face was clowning around with such insouciance, girlie, the sadness that sometimes rustles through our neighborhood collided with a torrent of nightingales and left louts dangling from the wings of cherubim, a dissolute carnival caught in a cloud.

internuncio

a messenger, agent, go-between

"I'm no mere internuncio, honey," replied the Grim Reaper to the baba playing for time. "I'm the message *and* the messenger, and if you don't clamber into that urn—and I mean pronto!—I'm tucking you under my cloak."

"I'm no mere internuncio, honey," replied the Grim Reaper to the baba playing for time. "I'm the message and *the messenger, and if you don't clamber into that urn—and I mean pronto!—I'm tucking you under my cloak."*

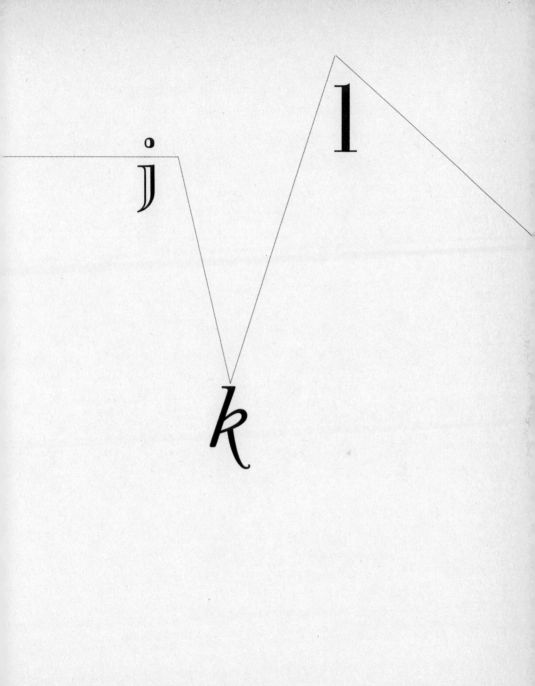

jeremiad

an elaborate and prolonged lamentation or tale of woe, written or spoken; from Jeremiah, the author of Lamentations

> When she came to her fifth decade, the contralto occasionally switched to a third-person narrative, which was a relief (to both her secretary and her readers) after all-too-frequent jeremiads over doomed liaisons, cruel critics, silly costumes, her rivals' tantrums; and it was thus that she presented her fiftieth birthday party, celebrated in Salzburg with such brio and opera buffa effects.

jeroboam

a wine bottle that holds four-fifths of a gallon, or 3.03 liters— named for the ancient king Jeroboam I of northern Israel

> Such birthday felicities had never befallen her! But on the eve of her fiftieth year, friends frocked from far and wide to toast her cockles, wish her some better ones, turn her over to the rosy hands of dawn. They festooned

her with pork butts and sackbuts, rounded off the evening and their profiles with sacher torte, and kept the jeroboams foaming at the mouths they opened to them, when they weren't plastering their kissers on the honored guest's.

juggernaut

an overwhelming advancing force that crushes or might crush everything in its path; an inexorable destructive force; also, a belief or institution demanding or eliciting blind or destructive devotion

> Arriving at "Former Employment, Previous Positions," on the apprenticeship application, Jonquil cast one confounding glance at the king's portrait before responding in her most adamant, steady hand: "A gentle, unflappable navigator on the waterways, a juggernaut in town."

kickshaw

a gewgaw, trinket, tsatskeleh, little treasure—or, if you want to eat it, a delicacy, *friandise*; *kickshaw* comes from French folk etymology: *quelque chose*, meaning "something"

> "You appraise the kickshaws behind the fake books of the library while I check out the boudoir for jewelry and tsatskelehs," adjured Nola while riffling through CDs of operas and cantatas and stuffing *Così Fan Tutte* down the front of her dress.

"*You appraise the kickshaws behind the fake books of the library while I check out the boudoir for jewelry and tsatskelehs,*" *adjured Nola while riffling through CDs of operas and cantatas and stuffing* Così Fan Tutte *down the front of her dress.*

laconic

concise, succinct, using few words

> Zoë Platgut recommends cutting out all adjectives ending in *-ous*, *-ic*, and *-escent* if you wish to fashion a laconic style of writing without dismantling your *Weltanschauung*, but her detractors dissuade her followers by casting aspersions on her truncheoned name.

lagniappe

What on earth does *lagniappe* mean? Could it be any or all of these?

- a sluggard who lies around till noon
- Provençal for "suburbanite"
- she-wolf of Anapurna
- the flutter presaging a migraine
- an empathetic ear
- a car that demands heavy pampering
- a debutante who eschews heavy petting
- Québecois pastry that's hard on the inside, floppy on the outside
- a row of winking buttons
- the step before the threshold

A commercial ritual in Louisiana, a *lagniappe* is something extra added to a purchase: a surprise handful of flour on a heap of homeward-bound grits, or the gratuitous flaskette of cologne coming along with a depilatory in a pearly paper shopping bag.

74

The word is pronounced *lan-yap*, the Creole French spelling having been laid over a word of Spanish and American Indian derivation.

Jacaranda returned home from the pizzeria with a lagniappe she could not countenance: a miniature aquarium swimming with live anchovies and sporting a simulated rock and bracken garden for ambiance: sprigs of rosemary and oregano, cloves of elephant garlic.

loquacity

talkativeness, garrulousness, volubility

Our interlocutor having quite flummoxed us with her deadpan, coy delivery and recondite replies, and our loquacity having in any case run its course and left us exhausted (we were utterly at a loss for words), we agreed to take a break for a day, a week, a year, from this elusive enterprise of talking back to the sphinx.

louche

disreputable, shady, dubious; from French, Old French: literally, cross-eyed, blind in one eye

As a Eurobanker since the collapse of the Soviet empire, Nimbo Moostracht deals with some mighty louche characters besides the ones he knows from college or those he summers with along the coruscating lakes and rivers of his native Azuriko— so naturally the investigators have quite a spate of suspects for these "brigands with fans" abducting his niece to the craters and crags of Trajikistan.

lubricious

lascivious, sexually aroused or obsessed; also, oily, slippery, tricky

The Asti Spumante sparkled in our spectacles; the antipasto deferred to the dessert course, refusing to arrive on time; our waiter, Torso, was topless and tremulous; while the focaccia was positively lubricious with truffles and virgin olives.

luminous

radiating or reflecting light; intellectually brilliant, enlightened or enlightening; clear and readily intelligible, as a trim and luminous dossier

> The lummox, his round face luminous, came thrashing through the bamboo thicket like a samurai in rut.

> His luminosity was notorious for elucidating the wherefores and likely upshots of massive discontent.

m

maelstrom

a turbulent or violent situation; tumult, turbulence, commotion;
an extraordinarily large or vigorous whirlpool; vortex

> "She's difficult to fathom, but what a way to drown!" he
> eulogized, moving on from the maelstrom of her cur-
> riculum vitae to her imponderable eyes.

malefic

having or exerting a malevolent, baleful influence; evil, malicious

> The lamia came at him amorously (and not malefically,
> as he at first supposed), twitching her tail, flashing her
> polychrome markings, twining herself around his legs,
> then slithering up over his waist and chest, and taking a
> good look into his open mouth before settling, encircled,
> like a crown on his head, the tapered end of her irides-
> cent tail draped decoratively over his left ear (which,
> from that time forward, she twiddled fondly when the
> impulse teased her).

m

maraud

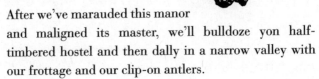

to raid, pillage for plunder; to rove
and raid in search of booty; from
French for tomcat, vagabond

> After we've marauded this manor
> and maligned its master, we'll bulldoze yon half-
> timbered hostel and then dally in a narrow valley with
> our frottage and our clip-on antlers.

marcel

a wavy hairdo, named for Marcel Grateau, a French coiffeur

> Celadonio waved to us from the departing train, his hair
> in wind-ruffled blue marcel ("my Marcel Proust," he
> called it, because of Proust's blue room), his large collar
> flopping as he leaned out to toss a bouquet of hyacinths
> at Roberto Abierto, his latest stuffed animal on the
> prowl.

marzipan

Marzipan has an involuted history commensurate with its cloy-
ing density. In this case, "to coin a word" is utterly apt. The
Teutons took it from the Italians, who were using *marzapane* to
box up another idea: a standard-sized container from an obso-
lete fine box for comfits and, to begin with, rare coins. But
before this, we go sailing backward to Arabia and Byzantium,
where *mawtaban* signified, respectively, a king on a throne and

a coin with Christ enthroned. Could this explain marzipan's rampant appearance in such countries as Holland, Germany, and Austria as Christmas and its packages arrive? Somehow sweets, treats, boxes, and Jesus all in three luscious syllables? My favorite use of *marzipan* in literature is by Sergei Dovlatov:

> . . . an unctuous, marzipanish person. A certain type: the timid manipulator.
>
> —*The Compromise*

maudlin

tearfully emotional, foolishly sentimental; also mawkishly sentimental from drunkenness, adrift on one's own tears in *le bateau ivre;* from the Greek version of Mary Magdalen, so often pictured weeping copious penitent tears

> The party was awash in gin fizzes and maudlin divulgences, and those who might have recalled what the others were bawling about had left them for an attractive back room.

ménage à trois

a romantic or domestic triangle; literally, a household of three

> "And this," she said, flinging open the master bedroom's garage door to reveal a small theater, "is our ersatz television, where we stage our mock-heroic couplings, Restoration comedies, and an occasional French farce featuring the neighborhood's latest ménage à trois and assorted dismembers of anyone's entourage."

meretricious

pertaining to or resembling a prostitute; attracting attention in
a vulgar manner; lacking sincerity

> I come to you with meretricious suggestions, beribboned
> smooches, dire predicaments, and imploring hands.

> . . . and he poured himself meretriciously into that trag-
> ic laugh of silver teeth.
>
> *—The Man in the Grey Flannel Suite*

mot juste

exactly the right word or expression

> So deafened with accolades was the chief brigand that
> his henchman Troto's *mot juste* whizzed right past his
> boutonniere.

mucilaginous

sticky, gummy, gelatinous, like mucus or glue

> Mein Schatz!
>
> Padding through the mush in our Schlaffenfuss
> gadabouts, we've spent our entire vacation in a very
> large bowl of oatmeal—a high-fiber resort, as it was
> touted in the brochure. Well, the gadabouts are really
> just high rubber boots (provided by the establishment as

they take away your money, your passport, and your clothes) that make these desperate sucking sounds each time a foot reaches toward the surface of this mucilaginous terrain.

Bye, see you soon, in your flimsy atmosphere, after we decompress for a few days in a vat of beet borscht.*

Love,

Yolanta

myriad

innumerable, multitudinous, composed of numerous diverse elements or facets; as a noun, a very large number

We rode the funicular to the entrance of Contrecoeur, the city below us scratching its myriad made-up eyes through a scarf of silky smog.

nacreous

having the quality, coruscation, or sheen of mother-of-pearl, which is also called nacre

Breakfasting alfresco before fully awake, Suzette spattered her nacreous negligee with café au lait when Incognito, her swain of the moment, mentioned a name she preferred to forget, a place she thought she'd fled forever, a memory of revolt and regret.

---

* Actually, after this they went on a Magyar safari, stalking the mild paprika in their Hungarian galoshes.

n

nefarious

infamously wicked, iniquitous, reprobate, nefast, unregenerate, outstandingly reprehensible, pernicious, odious

> The most nefarious beast for miles around was Deux Chevaux, a hoodwinked tomcat who lived in his mistress's handbag and sprang into action whenever she let him out of it. The handbag, it behooves me to divulge, was made of various animals Deux Chevaux had clawed to death in his ferocious, precocious kittenhood.

nemesis

a source of harm or ruin; retributive justice in its execution or outcome; an opponent that cannot be beaten or overcome

> That degenerate demagogue Joseph McCarthy met his nemesis when Edward R. Murrow met Milo Radulovich.

nimbus

In classical mythology, a shining cloud that sometimes surrounds a deity visiting Earth; cloud, aura, or atmosphere surrounding a person or thing; halo; rain-bearing cloud

> She kicked away off the barstool and glided out the door, a roseate nimbus of Campari and soda trailing after her.

The most nefarious beast for miles around was *Deux Chevaux*, a hoodwinked tomcat who lived in his mistress's handbag and sprang into action whenever she let him out of it. The handbag, it behooves me to divulge, was made of various animals *Deux Chevaux* had clawed to death in his ferocious, precocious kittenhood.

n

noblesse oblige

magnanimous, benevolent, honorable behavior considered to be the lot and responsibility of those born or ascended to high rank or class

> "Don't take that noblesse oblige tone with me!" countered the contralto's ghostwriter cum amanuensis, Nada Seria, offended by a feeling of déjà vu that smacked of *Figaro*, which made her the maid, and Constanza the contessa, messing around with her man.

noli me tangere

a warning against touching, prodding, meddling

> "This *noli me tangere* will get you nowhere," cautioned the career counselor through his handkerchief, top hat, and wire cage.

nostrum

a medicine—especially from a louche doctor or hawker of dubious concoctions—made of secret ingredients and touted with promises; a favorite but untested remedy for ailments or evils

> "You see, what I was seeking at that time, Nada, was an elixir for my *Weltschmerz*, a nostrum for my shaken confidence, a salvo of accolades from Spoleto and Vienna, and a pair of hairy arms to grab me in the cloakroom while I was rummaging about for my wrap," prefaced La Zermattress, hoping to soft-pedal the humiliations she was about to expose.

obstreperous

noisily and stubbornly defiant, aggressively boisterous; rambunctious, clamorous, rackety, roisterous

Hey, pal—

I'm gettin' tired of rustlin' the petticoats of cowboys, but before that happened, I got some great in flagrante delicto* snapshots, even a video—rituals, songs, lore of the laundromats—for my *Cowboys and Lingerie* monograph, soon to be an odd-Broadway musical. This particular moment finds me sitting at the edge of a bowl of quiet cucumber soup, but the waitresses are loudly clothed, and there's this obstreperous jukebox bellowing in the corner, so I think I'll clap on my flippers, fish the last macaroon out of my pocket, and see if there are stiller waters on the other side of the floor.

With love and lassoed garter belts,
Yolanta

* in flagrante delicto: in the very act, red-handed; literally, while the crime is blazing

O

*My next encounter at the pearly gates was
with an officious-looking angel who was
taking my measurements for wings.*

officious

excessively eager to offer unwanted advice or services; meddle-some, intrusive, overly solicitous

My next encounter at the pearly gates was with an offi-cious-looking angel who was taking my measurements for wings; recommending the continental breakfast (croissants, brioches baked by the Virgin herself, café au lait Mayakovsky, marmalade, honey, and unsweetened butter); interrogating me about my youthful indiscre-tions and the companions involved; auditioning me for the Hallelujah chorus; and buffing my fingernails, which I'd bitten unevenly on the way up, giving me a woebe-gone appearance quite out of keeping with the personal hygiene and dress codes that come with the turf in this precarious state of grace.

where the wings are made

O

on dit

a rumor or bit of gossip

There is a credible *on dit* circulating in the court that the prince is off his rocker.

orotund

pompous and bombastic; full in sound, sonorous

Rotund, orotund, and five foot six, Dante Kaputo was the Pavarotti of the Painted Desert, the Sancho Panza of the prairie, the pasha of the Pink Antlers Saloon.

oubliette

a secret dungeon with an opening only in the ceiling, often in a castle; from French, *oublier,* to forget, for one is left there to be forgotten

"You have one afternoon at the escritoire in which to finish this correspondence, my sweet, or it's off to the oubliette with you!" threatened Constanza, but her secretary was accustomed to this ersatz severity and called up her paramour to propose a quite different use of the desk.

outré

excessive, extreme; highly unconventional, bizarre

Don't you find these *soi-disant* exemplary sentences outré? I mean, no one actually talks this way!

"You have one afternoon at the escritoire in which to finish this correspondence, my sweet, or it's off to the oubliette with you!" threatened Constanza, but her secretary was accustomed to this ersatz severity and called up her paramour to propose a quite different use of the desk.

oxymoron

a figure of speech creating an incongruous, seemingly self-contradictory effect

> All the good-looking oxymorons are in love with me and come to visit me in my bed at night.
>
> —Charles Simic

Scenes from *The Forlorn Oxymoron*

She's positively staggering with poise

resilient gravity · · · · · · · · · · · · · · · disarmingly reassuring

a tasteful outrage

used mysteries

glibly tongue-tied · · · · · · · · · · · · uproariously docile

friendly cactus

a buoyant woe · · · · · · · · · · · · · twinkling darkly

slippery fastenings

tremulous bravado

jinxed charm

blatantly neutral

a monosyllabic chatterbox · · · · · · affably gruff

flamboyant modesty

sulky optimism

retarded speed demonry

94

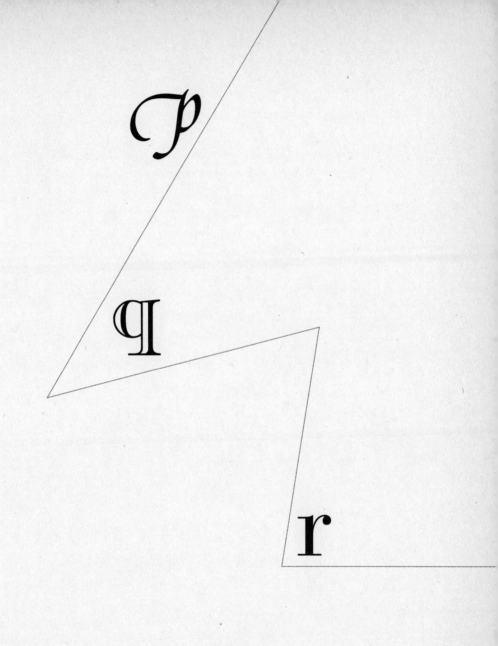

palaver

a long parley, conference, or discussion; profuse and idle talk; chatter; flattery, cajolery; from Portuguese, *palavro*, and from Latin, *parabola*, parable

> "Can't have too much of a good thing!" yapped Miranda when Mrs. Gallimauf asked her if she was set for another round of punch and palaver.

pander

to act as a go-between in a sexual escapade; to procure for sexual pleasure. See Pandarus in Chaucer's *Troilus and Criseyde*, turned into "Old Pimpsey" by one of my fellow Chaucer students in his pastiche on that Trojan War tale of love, its arrangements, and its betrayal. In the sense of catering to the base desires of others for exploitative purposes, *pander* is also used to describe the machinations of a market economy.

> That Bible Belter panders to the sleaziest hankerings and tawdriest afterthoughts when calling suckers and

sinners to his brimstone sheepfold padded with pornography and penitential dollars.

— *The Lambkins of Dreadmore Valley*

panegyric

a formal eulogistic composition intended as a public compliment; elaborate praise or laudatory carryings-on; an encomium

"The temperature is capricious" is how theater critic Cedric Moltgang summed up the dramatic progression of *Giovanna's Rheum,* after a fervent panegyric on the fuliginous* huskiness of Giovanna's voice.

par excellence

being the best or truest of a kind; exemplary; quintessential

Nimbo Moostracht, Eurobanker par excellence, spent the evening with his chauffeur studying the ransom note from every angle and pondering all possible quid pro quos they might propose to this ruthless band of brigands with fans and short-wave radios.

* fuliginous: sooty, covered with soot, and thus applied to Cinderella in *The Glasnost Slipper*

parvenu

one so suddenly risen in fortune or class that he or she has not yet been accepted by others on that recently attained level

> That parvenu in her affections has yet to grovel before her greyhound or suffer the scrutiny of her pet soubrette.

peccadillo

a slight flaw, sin, or transgression

> We were allowed three peccadilloes each throughout the evening—but who was to say what constituted an acceptable indiscretion, what an egregious* offense?

pelagic

of, relating to, or living in the open seas, not by the shore or on inland waterways

> This pelagic pas de deux was commandeered by the curator of Azuriko's National Gallery to replace the stolen masterpiece of Vole Incubyte, *Fishmonger Taking His Carp Back in a Huff.*

---

* egregious: remarkably bad; flagrant

p

penurious

mean, stingy, skinflinty; chintzy, niggardly, cheap; ungenerous-ly unwilling to spend money

> We're having an astringent and penurious Christmas this year—no presents, only one Wise Man (with frangi-pani, not frankincense, minus myrrh, and a tin crown upon his cranium), no balm of Gilead—although Jon-quil suggested she come as a shattered Salome and do the Dance of the Tatterdemalion.
>
> —*The Abduction of the Magi*

perambulation

a walk, promenade, stroll, saunter

> She returned from their brambly perambulation blithely innocent of the bloodsucker burrowed beneath her col-lar; three weeks later, the grand swoon seized her and flung her out of bed.

perfidious

treacherous, traitorous, faithless, double-crossing

> The mastodons would brook no nonsense from perfidi-ous proselytizers bent on wrecking the small joys they found at church bazaars and confessionals.

persiflage

light bantering talk or writing; a fripperous or flippant style of

treating a subject (from a French word for hissing and whis-
tling); badinage, raillery, waggery

> It's amazing how sometimes he struck, amidst his excel-
> lent persiflage, a chord of deep and heart-rending senti-
> ment.
>
> —Augustus John, of Ronald Firbank

perturbation

agitation, disturbance, inquietude, fretfulness, intense anxiety

> We could hardly wait to slough off our despondencies
> and resume our perturbations!
>
> —*The Weltschmerz Jumper*

philanderer

a casual lover and cruiser of possible conquests; someone who
philanders, of course

> She entered the waiting room and threw herself into a
> corner chair beside a potted philanderer.

> She had been mauled by a disgusting old philanderer
> when her breasts were not yet even buds.

And hark this howler!

> Freesias, snapdragons, or lobelia make a more tasteful
> bridal gift than a gawky philanderer delivered in a van.
>
> —*Giovanna's Mortgage*

pied-à-terre

an extra place to stay, usually in another town, and often smaller than one's usual house, without one's usual spouse; literally, foot on the ground

> "What I really need is two pied-à-terres, so I can keep one foot on each continent, then my mouth and body on my lover," mused Jonquil as she shuffled floor plans among the pages of her atlas.

plaudit

enthusiastic praise, and its expression in vociferous or gestural terms; accolade

> As a sophomore, she'd been a participant in a beauty queen contest and walked off with plaudits and a battery-lit tiara that was rechargeable, bright enough to read by, and grew thorns when she suspired.

plethora

an excessive amount,
a superabundance; surfeit, spate

> A plethora of possibilities
> crepitated in the spaces widened
> by their embraces; a mislaid word, a
> wrong foot, a curious touch, an ardent look
> could at any moment knock one of these into play.

poem

> A young poet once said to Mallarmé, "I had the most marvellous idea for a poem this afternoon." "Oh dear," said Mallarmé, "what a pity." "What do you mean?" said the young poet. "Well," said Mallarmé, "poems aren't made of ideas, are they? They're made of words."
> —Stephen Fry, *The Hippopotamus*

poltergeist

a ghost making its presence known through noises, rappings, and manifest disorder

> "That poltergeist you gave us as a wedding present prances around in our pajamas and raps with the rhythms of a Macedonian gypsy when we break out the slivovitz," wrote Laurinda to Loona after her honeymoon in Lavukistan.

poltroon

a wretched coward; a craven recreant

> He sent a gaggle of goggle-eyed poltroons to the dubious dwelling to sniff out which suspicion should be leveled as a charge.

portentous

foreboding, momentous, ominously significant; of unspecifiable significance, exciting wonder or awe; amazing, marvelous

> And what a portentous meeting it would prove to be. Already the boys on the back benches were greasing

their guns, journalists were sharpening their quills, spokesmen were subduing their qualms and preparing to mouth off with pugnacious* aplomb.

postprandial

after a meal, especially a dinner

These postprandial chats and preposterous assertions led to disembosoming interviews and further revelations that ultimately would topple both the penumbral palace and its *non compos mentis** prince.

priapic

phallic; overwrought or overly concerned with masculinity

"He's trying to photosynthesize me!" cries one of the nymphs who's turned herself into a tree to confound the attentions of a faun.

He adapts to the new form she's taken by spreading

* pugnacious: combative, belligerent, ready for a fight or looking for one
* *non compos mentis:* not mentally competent

out the contents of his priapic picnic basket* and having a leisurely midafternoon lunch and snooze in the ample shade the nymph's leafy limbs now offer in lieu of a struggled embrace.

—The Seventy Carnal Synonyms

prodigal

rashly or wastefully extravagant; *prodigal* can also be applied to things other than character and thereby mean lavish or profuse, in abundance

> The bosom of his family was not the soft landing he'd longed for; a VCR now wore his mother's apron (he was wearing his silver lamé prodigal sundress) and played him flashbacks of his feckless, squandered twenties.

prodigious

impressively great in size, force, extent; enormous; extraordinary, marvelous; taken to darker extremes, ominous

> There for a fortnight they did loll—a pair of chaise loungers basking in the prodigious sun, mooning when it was gone.

profligacy

squandering, extravagance, reckless spending and scattering

> "Oh, I rarely do anything for a single purpose—what a profligacy of my precious time and talents that would

---

* Priapic picnic basket comes with aphrodisiacs, erotic accoutrements, and satyr shoes—cloven hoofs, furry toes.

be!" bellowed the contralto in one more digression on her repertoire and raison d'être as Nada scratched out another five lines and suppressed an impudent riposte.

prolix

wordy, long-winded, verbose, pleonastic

"I've had enough of your euphonious expressions and prolix paragraphs!" protested the dummy, mouthing off for the first time in her muffled and muslined life.

propinquity

nearness, closeness, proximity

Meet me at the Palaz of Hoon somewhere in the propinquity of soon.

provenance

place of origin, derivation; proof of authenticity of a work of art or an antique

"The provenance of these tears you shall never discover, nor the fate of the heroine and her handkerchief!" warned a banner that fluttered tauntingly over the proscenium as the curtains disclosed the somber setting of *The Sorrows of Tristesse du Sanglot.*

pudenda

external genital organs of either sex, although more often female; *pudenda* alights in scenes here that countermand its original meaning of shame

"Am I crushing your pudenda?" she asked, fluffing up

106

"The provenance of these tears you shall never discover, nor the fate of the heroine and her handkerchief!" warned a banner that fluttered tauntingly over the proscenium as the curtains disclosed the somber setting of The Sorrows of Tristesse du Sanglot.

p

They call her the quasimodo showgirl: she boogies backwards, treads on the tables, thrusts her hips through the windows, raises the eyebrows of an earlier decade, and blows kisses to the putti serving Campari in the joint next door.

the space conjoining them, settling her weight over the chair's hairy forearm, and lapping up the droplets of pleasure still reflected in two of his eyes.

She scratched her pudenda coquettishly and fingered him out the door.

—The Seventy Carnal Synonyms

punctilio

a fine point of etiquette; precise observance of formalities; nicety, propriety

We paid obeisance to the most fatuous punctilio, then betook ourselves to a raunchy roadhouse for faux pas, pig feet, fox trots, and frosted mugs of Guinness stout.

putti

cupids that make themselves useful, as in the paintings of Nicolas Poussin, who left France to paint in Italy just so he could put these winged *bambini* to work for all his beautiful *donne*, holding their mirrors, combing their tresses, helping them into their underwear, bearing them trays of *dolci* like zabaglione and frangipane.

They call her the quasimodo showgirl: she boogies backwards, treads on the tables, thrusts her hips through the windows, raises the eyebrows of an earlier decade, and blows kisses to the putti serving Campari in the joint next door.

quodlibet

a subtle or elaborate argument or point of debate

 Pinioning his interlocutor with a quivering quodlibet, Cram Fossilblast extracted a feather from his waistcoat pocket and proceeded to titillate the poor fellow's syllogisms through the ensuing polemic.

raconteur

teller of tales; anecdoter of considerable skill, style, delivery, and wit

Alf Musket is one hell of a raconteur; even his hush puppies have gossip to monger.

raddled

worn out and broken-down

He led her off to a raddled sofa behind the ballroom footbath to sit in her lap and spin her mendacious tales of homeopathic penguins and Balanchine kangaroos.

recalcitrant

stubborn, defiant, obstinate, refractory, intractable, contumacious

Negotiations between the parties snagged when a recalcitrant ombudsman in midlife crisis skulked off with both the offers and kicked up a new cloud of strife.

He led her off to a raddled sofa behind the ballroom
footbath to sit in her lap and spin her mendacious
tales of homeopathic penguins and
Balanchine kangaroos.

r

recherché

exquisite, choice; excessively refined, precious; overblown, pretentious

> "That takes the solitary, unique, and, if I may so call it, recherché biscuit!"
>
> —James Joyce, "Two Gallants"

recidivous, recidivistic

relapsing to a former behavior pattern, usually criminal

> I'd like to present my desperado brother, but his latest recidivous capers have landed him in the slammer once again.

> I'll decaffeinate *you*, young lady, if it's my last act on this slaphappy, recidivistic earth!

recondite

not easily understood; abstruse; perplexing, complicated; cryptic, concealed, hidden, imperspicuous

> "Your daughter is the most recondite urchin ever to scrape her boots on the doormat of my classroom," wrote Zoë Platgut, Nola's kindergarten teacher, to that antiquated paterfamilias, a medieval scholar who'd raised his only child on a macaronic mélange of Latin,

Old French and Provençal, Old Norse, and Middle English.

recumbent

lying down with great comfort, even pleasure; reclining, couchant, supine, horizontal; resting, idle

> *Torpor in the Swing* is one of the most unmoving novels of recent times; the protagonist does little but blink and languidly turn the pages of *her* soporific bestseller, *The Wretch of Lugubria,* which we are obliged to read over her shoulder *aloud to her* while her soubrette massages her feet.

redolent

aromatic, scented, giving off fragrance; suggestive, evocative, reminiscent of

> The musk deer were waxing redolent: rutting season had begun.

> She was still in the "Oh, dear—what *shall* I wear?" stages of her preparations when he and his branches of jasmine came redolently through the door.
> —*The Stupor of Flanelle Lune*

refection

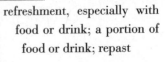

refreshment, especially with food or drink; a portion of food or drink; repast

We paused in the heat of our vituperations for a matinee at Café Frangipane: silk pajamas, barefoot recumbencies, and cool refections that kissed us into dulcifying our ires while serenaded by lutenists on shoplifted lyres.

repartee

a swift, witty reply; conversation carried on through an exchange of witty remarks; banter

The repartee went straight to her head before she could unlock her jaw and set her mouth in furious motion.

reticence

a standoffish, reluctant, shy, modest, hesitant sort of reserve or
qualm

> "I feel not the slightest reticence in avowing that I was
> unable to consummate any attraction or passion with-
> out crying 'Wolfie!' at the height of my pleasure, for
> Mozart is the consummate artist of all ages, the *puer
> aeternalis** of my playground, the match that set me
> crackling," confessed the contralto before resuming her
> recollections of *The Abduction from the Seraglio* as it
> had been staged in Blegue.

* eternal boy

r

*And so the time to rusticate her had come...
She returned three months later a chafed and
scruffy version of her city self: her hair a
scorched manger of straw, her hands rough-
ened from tugging on goats' teats and turnips,
her lexicon stuffed with loutish new words.*

116

riposte

a retort; a quick thrust with a sword or words; retaliatory action

> You think *you've* been wounded! I still haven't recovered from his radioed riposte about the cosmetic dentistry in my mordant wit and my epistemological harlotry.

rodomontade

pretentious bragging or boasting; bluster, bombast; from Italian, via French, referring to the arrogant Saracen Rodomonte, in *Orlando Innamorato* and *Orlando Furioso*

> Such is the tenor of his rodomontade: vainglorious exploits, gastronomic excess, and transsexual conquests.

rusticate

to go to or live in the country; to send to the country

> And so the time to rusticate her had come...She returned three months later a chafed and scruffy version of her city self: her hair a scorched manger of straw, her hands roughened from tugging on goats' teats and turnips, her lexicon stuffed with loutish new words.

salacious

lascivious, prurient; appealing to or arousing sexual desire

> The manuscript he was shaking his shaggy head over was a salacious subversion of the *OED*.

salient

projecting, jutting, protruding; strikingly conspicuous; prominent, pronounced; springing, jumping

> The incursion of his laughter into her delicate concentration caused her to skip several salient sentences upon which the ensuing delirium was based.

salubrious

beneficial, promoting health and well-being; salutary, roborant

> The salubrious effects of these harangues were not always immediately apparent to their cringing victims, who'd wind up boxing their own ears just to soften such tendentious pontifications and vociferous onslaughts of meaning.

S

sardonic

scornfully derisive, mocking; from Greek, *sardinias*, alluding to a Sardinian plant that, when eaten, was said to bring on convulsive laughter leading to death

Jonquil's report card was especially colorful when it came to her behavior in geography class: "Miss Mapp feigns rapt attention, but just when I think she's following my every word and cartographic elucidation, she poses a series of impertinently imponderable questions, tosses some chum a sardonic grin, snaps her gum or her garter belt, and traces maps of magical hinterlands on one of her so-called Wohnenskirts,* with arrows pointing to a sylvan glade here, a caravanserai there, a fountain, a meadow, an abyss, a toll road closed for repairs."

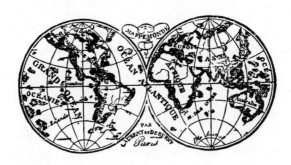

* Wohnenskirt: living-skirt. "It's the garment that accommodates my Liebensraum," she explained when she made her last wanderlusting presentation.

saturnine

melancholy or sullen in disposition; gloomy, glum, downcast, morose, sulky, blue; bitter, sarcastic

> Surrounded by the skulls of saturnine beings, she propelled herself dolefully into the future, prodding her fondest hopes and dreams into incorrigible acts of contrition.

Scaramouch, also Scaramouche

a stock character in old Italian comedy and pantomime, played as a braggart and buffoon

> Gregor Schlaffenfuss is surely the Scaramouch of the fashion industry this season, with his Alexanderplatzian hankies and Wombat Fatigues, his ubiquitous nightgowns on the town—from the supine to the vertiginous.

Schadenfreude

malicious joy at another's suffering or misfortune

> Once word of his niece's abduction had traveled, Nimbo Moostracht received six cards and notes of unmistakably *Schadenfreudian* import from his Eurobanking rivals in Louvelandia and Blegue.

S

scrag

a scrawny, bony person or animal; a piece of
lean or bony meat, especially neck of mutton

> We polished off the scrags and
> crusts on our plates and kicked
> back with our anecdotes and
> tobacco accoutrements.

> Then we came to a large scrag in the
> landscape, and there was no way to surmount
> it, so we took out our Swiss Army knives and sawed and
> gnawed away at it till only jutting bones remained.

scrofulous

affected with scrofula (a kind of tuberculosis); morally degener-
ate, corrupt

> He had a gorgeous succubus; she had a scrofulous
> incubus.

sedulous

diligent, persevering, assiduous; persistently or carefully main-
tained. From Robert Louis Stevenson comes an expression for
meticulously studying/copying another's style, Stevenson hav-

ing written that he had "played the sedulous ape to Hazlitt, to Lamb, to Wordsworth . . ."

Flaumina Untergasser had long played the sedulous* ape to such fashion luminaries as Nono Rockiano, Curl Rhineblaut, Alfonsi Lombardini, and Ghislain Douxveau before hitting her stride on the runways of Paris and Milan with her Sumptuary Outlaw collection.

seraglio

a well-endowed harem, and its dwelling place, and the setting for one of Mozart's operas; a sultan's palace

Aside from the luminous lyricism imparted by her Emily Dickinson nail polishes and lipsticks (Quiet Quartz on Amber Shoe, Whizz Triumphant, Gypsy Face Transfigured, to name a few), Foxy Belle Bloom's boudoir looked like a cross between a hairdresser's for rejects from Dante's *Inferno* and a tawdry scrap of seraglio torn from a time-share in Constantinople.

* *And* hirsute: her coiffeur had to take on those forearms along with the hair on her head.

S

simulacrum

an image or representation of something; an unreal or vague semblance of something

> "Is this a simulacrum, or was it stripped from a stalked and slaughtered lynx?" asked Lada Larkovich, a look of *Weltschmerz* darkening her face as she solicitously stroked the lustrous fur of the proffered coat.

skirl

any shrill sound, from a bagpiping term; as a verb, *skirl* means to shriek, if no bagpipes are making the sound for you. *Skirling* can also refer to a movement, rather like swirling.

> "Someone's nicked my knickers!" skirled Fiona O'Flimsie, her shoes dancing on her castoff breastplate, her eyes made up to spell alarm.

soi-disant

self-styled, so-called

> "That *soi-disant* diva was really just a trollop with a two-bit frog in her throat!" impugned Constanza of the little maestro's sidekick, whose vibrato he'd saved from the bottle, whose soft tread he'd recalled to the stage.

soigné, or soignée

showing sophisticated elegance, fashionable; well groomed, polished

> We kissed the hooves of the Henri IV statue's horse, brayed our "*Bonne soirée!*"s to the Napoleon in its belly,

"Is this a simulacrum, or was it stripped from a stalked and slaughtered lynx?" asked Lada Larkovich, a look of Weltschmerz *darkening her face as she solicitously stroked the lustrous fur of the proffered coat.*

S

then boogied the night away in a soignée *boîte de nuit* off la place Dauphine.

solipsism

the philosophical theory or view that the self is the only thing that can be known and verified, that it is the only reality

> Why do not all women enrapture themselves in slips? What silken sensations they are missing from this castoff undergarment, this hidden dentellated demi-exoderm that might slide softly between flesh and dress, creating another reality against the visible one, a sensuous solipsism with which a woman can comfort herself as she confronts the world.
>
> —*To Die in a Dirndl*

sotto voce

in an undertone; in soft tones, so as not to be overheard

> Roisterously and Rolls-Roycingly, Moostracht rolled up into the scenery of her sotto voce life.

soupçon

hint, tinge, suspicion

> A soupçon of raffishness clung to his tumbler as he mopped up the spilled contents of his misogynistic tale.

spumescent

I made this one up, out of *spume:* foam or froth on a liquid; as a verb, it means to foam or froth

Our Cucina Futurista banquet ended with a spumescent zabaglione served by cupids (sporting eye patches, horns) who hovered through the dessert with cigarettes and matches, poised for the newspaper-shredding course.

S

spurious

lacking authenticity or validity in essence or origin; false

> "Spuriouser and spuriouser" is how Alice would have dismissed most of the *Wonderland* and *Looking-Glass* dissertations that delved too deeply or recklessly into Dodgson's photographic predilections for Victorian little girls.

stricken

wounded; overwhelmingly affected by pain or trouble; incapacitated, disabled

> There were all these stricken faces and wrenched torsos lining her hallway of gilded lilies and full-length mirrors.

succès d'estime

critical success; acclaim from professional critics; an artistic work receiving such acclaim, often without commensurate financial gain

> Flaumina Untergasser's Sumptuary Outlaw collection was the *succès d'estime* of the season, but her emerald bustiers, ruby stigmatas (bracelets and anklets worn not on the wrists and ankles, but on the palms and the soles of the feet), diamond swizzle sticks, and seven-inch gold collars were dismissed by Severo Trobalini in the *International Herald Tribune* fashion supplement: "Fools rush in where angels wouldn't be caught dead."

susurration

a muffled mouthful, whisper

> Oh, send one of your susurrations over this way, baby, and make me come closer to hear it!
> *—Anatomy of a Murmur*

sybaritic

given or devoted to pleasure, even excessively so; hedonistic, voluptuous, self-indulgently sensuous

> And so the two sybaritic septuagenarians stripped down to their *Strumpfhosen* and sank into the sumptuous (but waterless) tub—well, the young puppy of a clerk didn't know whether to avert his gaze or climb in with them, just to clinch the sale.

syncope

a brief loss of consciousness (oxygen depletion, transient anemia); a swoon

> Sharing a syncope on the shaded edge of the Holy Spirit Crab Feed were a teenager from Tasco (who conversed nightly with Fluriel, the Angel of Youthful Confusion) and a Rosicrucian piglet all forlorn, just possibly a promising convert.

S

The objects that ride around in our pockets, that slumber in our desks, are all seen as companions by Jean-Jacques Passera, and also as testimonies of mood. "There might be a hidden bomb in a toothbrush; it could take revenge on you," he says with a reassuring self-composure.

terpsichorean

of or relating to dancing; from Terpsichore, the
Greek muse of dancing and choral singing

> This terpsichorean timepiece is no stranger
> to the tango, and breaks into a jitterbug
> at the oddest moments of its face.

thaumaturge

a magician, necromancer, sorcerer, worker of miracles

> His eyes look as if they have just pounced on something
> (that you didn't even see) and given it (whatever it was)
> new significance in this sudden embrace. He looks at
> some ordinary object, taking in an impression of its pos-
> sible necessity, but also wondering if it has a soul. The
> object is in captivity, the oppressions are immense. A
> poseur of questions and a thaumaturge, Jean-Jacques
> takes it, with its shimmering encumbrances, and helps it
> find something to do. A day might be poured into a
> thimble. A clothespin might become a ship. The objects
> that ride around in our pockets, that slumber in our
> desks, are all seen as companions by Jean-Jacques
> Passera, and also as testimonies of mood. "There might
> be a hidden bomb in a toothbrush; it could take revenge
> on you," he says with a reassuring self-composure.
>
> — "Several Crucial Moments of Jean-Jacques Passera,
> and Some Very Rich Hours, Too"

titivate

to make decorative additions to; to spiff up; as an intransitive verb, *titivate* means to gussy oneself up

> The pied-à-terre she keeps in Rome includes a gigolo to press her pants, palpate her remote control, and titivate her terrazzo.

troglodyte

a cave dweller; figuratively, a person who is seen as reclusive, out of date, reactionary, farouche

> Remember that chasmophile having a *crise* of stage fright back when this book began? Well! What should she do but creep into the soul of a strapping troglodyte, swear her undying domestication, and tack her doormat to his closet floor!

trousseau

a woman's possessions such as clothing and linen that accompany her into marriage; connubial accoutrements; the chattel of a bride

> She arranged her trousseau amongst a basket of langoustes and showed up at her shower wearing a pair of antlers she'd nabbed from some bloke in a bar.

134

She arranged her trousseau amongst a basket of
langoustes and showed up at her shower
wearing a pair of antlers she'd
nabbed from some bloke
in a bar.

truckle

to be servile or submissive; to cultivate someone's favor through obsequious and submissive behavior; to fawn, bootlick, kowtow

> While I trifled with his feelings, he truckled to my auntie and ate caramels from her crystal ball.

truculence

a disposition to fight, and fiercely; ferociously cruel actions or behavior

> Reading such works by Garland Slattersly as *The Battered Bride, Giovanna's Mortgage*, and *The Girl with the Golden Eyesore*, one wonders what private principle of mysogynistic truculence compels this author to present his tragic heroines in such an abusive, unflattering light.

tryst

a rendezvous, appointment, meeting, often with lascivious intent

> Suggesting a tryst and naming the place (Le Petit Auberge des Deux Hugos), she added, with a raffish

slant to her handwriting, "Well, what shall it be this time—politesses or fervor?"

tumulus

an ancient grave mound; a barrow

"Vargas Scronx's literary criticism is little more than a desecrated tumulus of unremarkable, unremarking aperçus and mean-spirited academic ax-grindery," intoned his contender for the Tory Auslander chair of Amplochacha U—whose own output, written under the nom de plume Strophe Dulac, included *The Emerald Settee* and *Tatiana's Bear.*

turgid

swollen or distended, fluidly so; bloated, you might say; excessively ornate in style or language; grandiloquent

Their ankles turgid from long working hours on their feet, the lady riveters donned cowboy boots, luring the stray admirer's eye to a herd of neat little calves.

— *The Glasnost Menagerie*

Nothing like the turgid prose of a fawning conquistador to make the blood rush through her lace, her heart to leap into a rosy inferno where such words would have no dominion.

tzigane

a gypsy, and a Hungarian one in particular; as an adjective, of or pertaining to gypsies

Le Petit Auberge des Deux Hugos was jangling with *tziganes,* who made off with the moonlight and the curtains *and* the sunrise before dawn.

"The world is my bedroom," read the ravenous
bodice of her ubiquitous nightgown,
"— I only sleep socially."

ubiquitous

omnipresent; being or seeming to be everywhere at once

> "The world is my bedroom," read the ravenous bodice of her ubiquitous nightgown, "—I only sleep socially."

umbrage

offense, resentment; shadow, shade, or something that provides them

> Tall, dark, mustachioed Mediterranean male seeks lithe, blithe strawberry blonde for walks and rumpled hairdos. Likes simple home cooking (in neither your home nor mine: for this we invade alien territory). Gives good umbrage.

unbosom

to confide, reveal one's thoughts and feelings; to relieve oneself of troublesome thoughts and feelings

> "That sloe-ginned mama in her marinated muumuu is about to unbosom a flow of indiscretions and bring blushes to the tips of our antlers," cautioned one marauder to another taking refection at Blotto Junction.

u

unctuous

having the quality or characteristics of oil or ointment; greasy, lubricious; characterized by affected, exaggerated, or insincere earnestness; ingratiating

> Honeyed phrases failing to have the desired effect (his total capitulation), Laurinda slipped into such an unctuous oration (while greasing his palm, as the guidebook had suggested) that, while not comprehending a word of this fawning foreigner, the customs official stamped her passport and waved her on into Lavukistan, his obdurate stance quite bootless on this lubricious verbal terrain.

verity

truth, truthfulness; quality of being factual or real; also, a statement, belief, or principle thus characterized, especially enduringly so, in someone's mind, anyway

> I mangled among the other guests, clucking appreciatively at their hoary anecdotes, splaying my fingers in mock protestation, dilating my pupils in genuine horror, owning the verity of each proffered compliment; and if the smallest indecency poked its snout through the muddle of someone's monologue, I would hasten to compose my features into a picture of doelike innocence before bounding off into a bowl of punch.
>
> — *The Glass Shoe*

*I would hasten to compose my features into a
picture of doelike innocence before
bounding off into a bowl
of punch.*

vicissitude

change or variation; successive, alternating, changing phases or conditions, such as ups and downs; mutation, mutability

> Over the years I've painted my rooms to match my mood, my *mode de vie*, my passions and vicissitudes, always naming the colors myself, after mixing the paints and the metaphors: my carefree, tawny twenties in *Tiepolo, Dusting the Credenza, Steals Some Cookies*, then *Calvados on the Double*; the lovelocked room of *Under My Rhinebeau*; the misted mauve I called *Maud Gonne, Get Out of the Sun*; a frisky violet wingtip called *Zephyr Laughing Gently at the Canterbury Pilgrims*; and the latest lavender of them all, mirror murmuring on the wall — a spirit summoned from the Coast of Sorrows, cracking the windows and flooring my ceilings: *Life Is Too Big Without You.*

virulent

actively poisonous, noxious
(as a virulent snake—or lamia—bite);
malignant; violently or spitefully
hostile; intensely bitter, spiteful

> A virulent wind had been
> stirring up trouble for days,
> evincing deeds of destruc-
> tion and snarls of distemper
> before flattening the coliseum
> and whipping the velveteen rabble
> into a sumptuous delirium.
>> —*Out of the Loud Hound of Darkness*

vituperation

sustained, harshly abusive language; invective; ferocious cen-
sure

> She was like a vituperation
> In the mouth of July.
> Only her feet touched sometimes the ground,
> Only my hands asked her why.
>> — *"Blaze On, My Little Tumbleweed,"*
>> as sung by Jusko Bou Trompe

voluble

flowing with speech; talkative, loquacious, garrulous

> Throughout the interview he waxed so voluble with rodomontade that they suspected a checkered career and prison record for con artistry, not the milk toastery that had actually flavored his recently dejected comportment.

vortex

a whirling, spiraling mass of water or other liquid that sucks everything near it toward its center; a situation or place that draws into its center all that surrounds it, or exerts such a curious force that it is regarded as doing so

> I found myself plunged into a vortex of words, burning words, cleansing words, liberating words, feeling words, and the words were all ours, and it was enough that we held them in our hands to play with them; whatever you can play with is yours, and this was the beginning of knowing.
>
> —Gertrude Stein

wafture

the act of waving; a wave of the hand, not of the sea

> And then, after all these waftures had settled down and the gathering had come to order, an indiscreet question-

naire made its way from row to row, and some low whistles stirred the skirts.

—*Twenty-two to Tea*

wamble

to move in a weaving, wobbling, or rolling manner; an unsteady or rolling movement

She wambled forth and calcified.

Weltanschauung

a comprehensive concept or image of the universe and of humanity's relation to it; literally, world-view

Oh, baby, take me into your *Weltanschauung*, and may it totter without me!

Weltschmerz

sadness over the evils of the world; brooding woefulness; a romantic pessimism, a Black Forest of sorrow; literally, world-pain

"This *Weltschmerz* is most becoming, my bountiful cry-baby."

She twists the tears out of her fichu and wails, "Alas, I have more where these come from!"

—*The Sorrows of Tristesse du Sanglot*

words

Ah, but I love to draw beautiful words, like trumpets of light....I adore you, words who are sensitive to our sufferings, words in red and lemon yellow, words in the steel-blue color of certain insects, words with the scent of vibrant silks, subtle words of fragrant roses and seaweed, prickly words of sky-blue wasps, words with powerful snouts, words of spotless ermine, words spat out by the sands of the sea, words greener than the Cyrene fleece, discreet words whispered by fishes in the pink ears of shells, bitter words, words of fleurs-de-lis and Flemish cornflowers, sweet words with a pictorial ring, plaintive words of horses being beaten, evil words, festive words, tornado and storm-tossed words, windy words, reedy words, the wise words of children, rainy, tearful words, words without rhyme or reason, I love you! I love you!

—James Ensor, Belgian artist

wunderkind

a person of astonishing talent or ability who is already an accomplished phenomenon at an early age; a child prodigy

"The most miraculous wunderkind of all time, Wolfgang Amadeus Mozart, shall remain the raison d'être of each breath I draw till my coloratura wears black," concluded the memoirs of Constanza Zermattress, the contralto from Amplochacha.

Jonquil's Map of
Word Origins

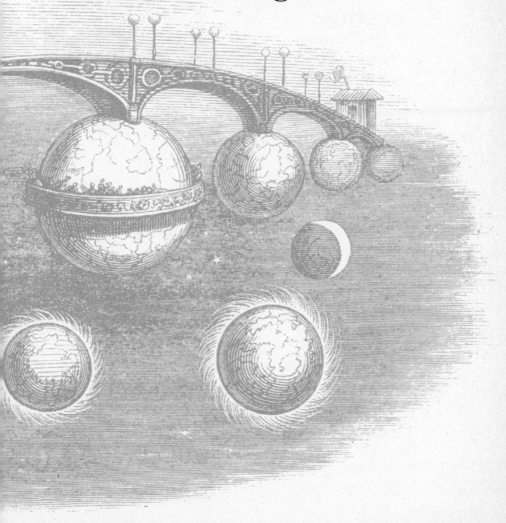

Arabic

nacreous (via Italian and French)

Celtic

feckless (Scottish)
flummery (Welsh)
skirl (Scottish, but, earlier yet,
    Scandinavian)

Dutch

fraught
maelstrom
scrag

French

accolade	coiffure
amour-propre	coterie
aperçu	coup de grâce
avoirdupois	crepuscular
boudoir	(from Latin)
boutonniere	cupidity (from Latin)
brouhaha	décharné
cabriole	décolletage
cache	déjà vu
calèche	demure
camisole	depravity
charivari, shivaree	divertissement
claque	dossier
coiffeur	doyenne

152

effrontery
(from Latin)
éminence grise
ensellure
entourage
escritoire
esplanade
(from Italian,
from Latin)
folderol
fripperous
frottage
gambado
gigolo
hauteur
idiot savant
insouciance
kickshaw
louche
maraud
marcel
ménage à trois
mot juste
noblesse oblige
on dit
oubliette
outré

paramour
par excellence
parvenu
persiflage
pied-à-terre
politesse
poltroon
raconteur
raison d'être
repartee
riposte
Scaramouch
(from Italian)
soi-disant
soigné, soignée
soubrette
soupçon
succès d'estime
trousseau
tryst
(from German,
Gothic)
umbrage (from Old
French, Latin)
urchin
verity (from Old
French, Latin)

German

Bildungsroman
Doppelgänger
ersatz
famulus (from Latin)
poltergeist
sacher torte, or Sacher torte
Schadenfreude
Weltanschauung
Weltschmerz
wunderkind

GREEK

amaranthine
anodyne
anomalous
antidote
apotheosis
chasmophile
chthonic
diatribe
draconian
halcyon
haptic
hubris
laconic
maudlin
myriad
nemesis
oxymoron
panegyric
philanderer
priapic
sardonic
sedulous (probably)
sybaritic
syncope
terpsichorean
troglodyte

Hebrew
jeremiad
jeroboam

Hindi
juggernaut

ITALIAN
aficionado
alfresco
belladonna
bordello
    (from Old French)
cicerone
cognoscente, -i
credenza
dolce far niente
fantoccini
frangipani
inamorata
internuncio
punctilio
putti
rodomontade
Scaramouch
stiletto
terrazzo

155

LATIN

amanuensis
amplitude
approbation
asseverate
cachinnate
calumniate
castigate
catalepsy
compunction,
    compunctious
concatenation
concupiscence
consanguine,
    consanguineous
contrite
crepuscular
    (via French)
cupidity
denizen
    (via Anglo-Norman)
depravity
despondency
desultory
diffidence
disconsolate
divagation

dulcify
effrontery
    (via French)
evince
exhort
expurgate
extirpate
famulus
    (via German)
fatuous
formication
fractious
frangible
fripperous
    (via French)
fulgurant
genius loci
gregarious
hirsute
ignominious
imminent
imprecation
imputation
ineluctable
ineptitude
in extremis

in flagrante delicto
ingenuous
innocuous
lascivious
loquacity
lubricious
luminous
malefic
mucilaginous
nebulous
nefarious
nimbus
noli me tangere
nostrum
obstreperous
officious
pelagic
penurious
perambulation
perfidious
perspicuous
perturbation
plaudit
portentous
postprandial
preposterous
prodigal

prodigious
profligacy
prolix
propinquity
provenance
pudenda
quodlibet
raucous
recalcitrant
recidivous,
    recidivistic
recondite
recumbent
redolent
    (via French)
refection
reticence
rusticate
sagacious
salacious
salient
salubrious
saturnine
scrofulous
simulacrum
solipsism
sotto voce

LATIN, *continued*

spumescent
  (via Old French)
spurious
susurration
tendentious
tenebrous
truckle
truculence
tumulus
turgid
ubiquitous
umbrage
  (via Old French)
unctuous
verity
  (via Old French)
vicissitude
virulent
vituperation
vivacious
voluble
  (via Old French)
vortex

Persian

pajamas
seraglio (via Turkish,
  Vulgar Latin,
  Italian)

Yiddish

tsatskeleh,
also tchotchkeleh
  (diminutive of tsatske,
  tchotchke)

Text Acknowledgments

Guy Davenport, on *crepuscular* and Noah Webster, from "More Genteel than God," in *Every Force Evolves a Form*. North Point Press, San Francisco, copyright © 1987 by Guy Davenport.

Sergei Dovlatov, line from *The Compromise*, translated from the Russian by Anne Frydman. Alfred A. Knopf, New York, 1983.

James Ensor, from *Ensor* by Paul Haesaerts, translated from the French by Norbert Guterman. Copyright © 1957 by Les Editions et Ateliers d'Art Graphique Elsevier, Paris and Brussels. Published in the United States in 1959 by Harry N. Abrams, New York.

Stephen Fry, passage from *The Hippopotamus*. Random House, New York. Copyright © 1994 by Stephen Fry.

Augustus John, line about Ronald Firbank, from Osbert Sitwell's introduction to Ronald Firbank's *Five Novels*. New Directions, New York, 1949. Introduction copyright 1950 by Sir Osbert Sitwell.

James Joyce, line from "Two Gallants," *Dubliners*. From the edition first published by Grant Richards, London, 1914.

Illustration Sources
and Acknowledgments

Thanks to Irene Bogdanoff Romo for help
in preparing these images.

Thomas Bewick: *Vignettes.* Copyright © 1978 by Scolar Press.

Stella Blum: *Victorian Fashions and Costumes from "Harper's Bazaar," 1867—1898.* Copyright © 1974 by Dover Publications, Inc.

Rikki Ducornet: Flying, flowing sphinx for *loquacity,* printed with permission of the artist, who is also the author of several miracles.

Jean-Ignace-Isidore Gérard (Grandville): *Fantastic Illustrations of Grandville.* Copyright © 1974 by Dover Publications, Inc.

Charles C. Gillispie: *A Diderot Pictorial Encyclopedia of Trades and Industry,* volume II. Copyright © 1959, 1987 by Dover Publications, Inc.

Carol Belanger Grafton: *Love and Romance.* Copyright © 1989 by Dover Publications, Inc.

——: *3,800 Early Advertising Cuts.* Copyright © 1991 by Dover Publications, Inc.

Jim Harter: *Animals: A Pictorial Archive from Nineteenth-Century Sources.* Copyright © 1979 by Dover Publications, Inc. *Harter's Picture Archive for Collage and Illustration.* Copyright © 1978 by Dover Publications, Inc. *Music: A Pictorial Archive of Woodcuts and Engravings.* Copyright © 1980 by Dover Publications, Inc. *Women: A Pictorial Archive from Nineteenth-Century Sources.* Copyright © 1978 by Dover Publications, Inc.

Johann Georg Heck: *The Complete Encyclopedia of Illustration.* Copyright © 1979 by Park Lane, Crown Publishers, Inc.

Clarence P. Hornung: *Handbook of Early Advertising Art.* Copyright 1947 by Clarence P. Hornung. Copyright 1953 and © 1956 by Dover Publications, Inc.

Richard Huber: *Treasury of Fantastic and Mythological Creatures.* Copyright © 1981 by Dover Publications, Inc.

Olja Invanjiki: Image of the nefarious beast Deux Chevaux, from *Knjiga o Olji.* Knjizevne Novine, Beograd, 1984.

Ernst Lehner: *Symbols, Signs and Signets.* Copyright 1950 by Ernst Lehner.

Ernst and Johanna Lehner: *Picture Book of Devils, Demons, and Witchcraft.* Copyright © 1971 by Dover Publications, Inc.

Drago Rastislav Mrazovac: Dress for doe-faced ingenue and the image of Constanza Zermattress, the contralto from Amplochacha, as well as the author portrait.

Jean-Jacques Passera: Toothbrush for the thaumaturge, Jean-Jacques himself.

Eleanor Hasbrouck Rawlings: *Decoupage: The Big Picture Sourcebook.* Copyright © 1975 by Dover Publications, Inc.